# MONSOON

# ASMA KHAN

# MONSOON

Delicious Indian recipes for every day and season

DK

[RED]

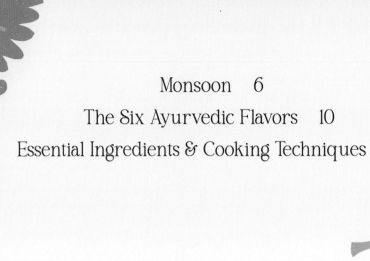

# MONSOON

The first time I saw a drizzle in England, I realized that I was really far away from home—far away from my beloved monsoon rain. It wasn't just the rhythm of the rain that was different—the water didn't linger on the leaves like it did in India, the rain in England came and went without the petrichor fragrance, which always followed a monsoon shower. I missed the excited calling of the birds, which signaled the rain was coming. The most beautiful sound was the call of the peacock, which would usually be shrill and grating, but when it rained you knew, hidden among the leaves, they had spread out their feathers and were dancing. It felt as if the earth was celebrating. The long summer months had parched the earth and finally nature was watering its garden. All the leaves were washed and sparkled like precious stones in the sunshine once the rainfall relented. This book is an homage to all the seasons, but the monsoons in India hold an almost spiritual significance for me. It was when the world stopped and nature displayed its benevolence through rain.

There is a uniqueness in the way we divide seasons in Bengal. Instead of the traditional spring, summer, fall, and winter seasons seen in many parts of the Western world, Bengali seasons ebb and flow poetically with nature. The seasons dictate the way we weave flavors into our food. The fruits and vegetables in the bazaar and on our dining table told a story of these changing seasons, and my childhood experience of seasonal cooking and eating is embedded in my foundations as a chef. Divided into six chapters, each chapter tells the story of the foods we ate in my family home over *Grishsho* (গ্রীষ্ম/Summer), *Bôrsha* (বর্ষা/Monsoon), *Shôrot* (শরৎ/Fall), *Hemonto* (হেমন্ত /Dry Season), *Sheet* (শীত/Winter) and *Bôshonto* (বসন্ত /Spring).

## THE SIX SEASONS OF FLAVOR

The soul of my cooking is the symphonic layering of vibrant flavors that work together like instruments in an orchestra. In India, we do not have a tradition of "meat and two veg," where every bite of an entire meal tastes the same. We use spices to bring in contradictory flavors, and different cooking techniques to highlight or accentuate a particular flavor. Salt is used in different ways to change the texture or cooking method of an ingredient. There are rituals, stories, and spirituality in our ancient culinary tradition.

The six Ayurvedic flavors define our culinary heritage: sour, tangy/astringent, spicy/pungent, sweet, salty, and bitter. The most satisfying meal is the one that stimulates as many of the six flavors in our palate as possible. A well-balanced meal should incorporate at least two elements of these to create a harmonious and stimulating dining experience. A perfect balance of flavors comes from contrasts: a touch of bitterness or sweetness, an astringent finish to a meal, or a refreshing tang midway through—not as a separate course, like a sorbet in fine dining, but as part of a flavorful, cohesive meal. Even the simplest Indian dishes are far from uniform.

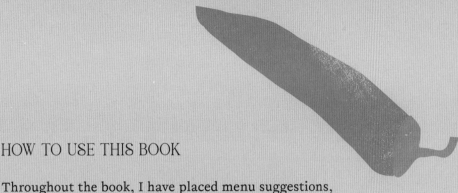

## HOW TO USE THIS BOOK

Throughout the book, I have placed menu suggestions,
followed by their constituent recipes. These meal
suggestions range from simple suppers to nourish
your soul, to sweet treats to accompany a match-day
gathering, to sumptuous feasts for special occasions,
and blend the Ayurvedic flavors in a harmonious way
to make ideal combinations. They are, of course, just
ideas. Once you feel confident with combining flavors,
you can create your own menus. Remember, all the
recipes in this book are just guides. The best recipes,
I feel, are the ones you create yourself by tweaking
my instructions to satisfy your own taste.

   Cooking is much like composing music. Once you've
mastered the basics, the artistry comes from trusting
your instincts and allowing yourself to create freely.
The most important ingredients in any dish are your
time, your personal touch, your sensibilities, and your
love. There's a deep emotional connection between you
and the person you're feeding, even if that person is
yourself. If nothing else, this book aims to equip you
with the fundamentals you need to express yourself
and nourish your soul through food. The recipes are
for any occasion, from midweek meals to special feasts.
I also hope that there will always be a go-to recipe for
every kind of day: sunshine or rain.

   This book celebrates the tapestry of flavors that are
interwoven into our food. I hope the suggestions for
combining ingredients inspire you to experiment
with different cuisines and enhance your meals by
thoughtfully incorporating spices. I welcome you with
open arms and heart. Let me take you on a flavor odyssey.

# The Six
# Ayurvedic Flavors

In Ayurveda, food has long been viewed as medicine, with spices considered healing agents. This philosophy centers on nourishing the body and soul through wholesome ingredients. Some spices, like turmeric, have antibacterial and anti-inflammatory properties, while others, like fennel seeds, aid digestion. My focus in this book is on cooking tasty food first and foremost, but I think the Ayurvedic framework of flavors is extremely valuable in classifying the bewildering array of Indian flavor combinations.

## Sour

This is the flavor that tingles your taste buds and moistens the palate. Often, we use a squeeze of lemon or lime juice, a splash of vinegar, or a smattering of pomegranate seeds on a salad without even thinking. Somehow, it just makes a dish taste better.

Yogurt is probably the most common souring ingredient used in India. Every region has its own version of a spiced, cooling, yogurt-based accompaniment, which is eaten on its own or mixed with other ingredients like cucumber, fresh tomatoes, fried eggplant slices, fresh herbs, and even grated fresh coconut. Other frequently used sour flavors in India are tamarind, lime, and lemon. Some sour fruits, such as kokum (which is similar to cranberries in flavor and related to the mangosteen family), are available in limited geographical areas like Goa and Maharashtra in Western India, and Kerala and Karnataka in South India. You should feel free to experiment and use local or indigenous sour fruit from your region to flavor your dish.

Another of the most common sour elements in many Indian meals comes from pickles. These can range from pickles with vinegar in them to sour berries and olives that are preserved in mustard oil and salt. The simplest of foods can be lifted with a bit of pickle on the side. My favorite combination is plain paratha with a dollop of plain yogurt and a pickle—it is such a deeply satisfying combination.

# Tangy
# (or Astringent)

A zingy, tangy flavor in any dish is like a ray of sunshine. This is a flavor that is often seen as a palate cleanser, as it strips the palate of moisture and prepares it for new flavor sensations. This dryness in the palate is sometimes described as chalkiness and it is a really important step in the process of how we taste and enjoy flavors. Remember: an astringent dish does not need to make you pucker up! Indian flavors will always be subtle and layered to bring structure to a meal.

Turmeric is one of the most interesting spices with attributes of tanginess (although it has attributes of other flavors too, such as pungency, sourness, and even bitterness). Lemons, limes, and other citrus fruits can also fall into two categories: tangy and sour. You will find these ingredients in all those dishes that are considered astringent in flavor, even if they also contain other spices and ingredients that may have more than one flavor profile.

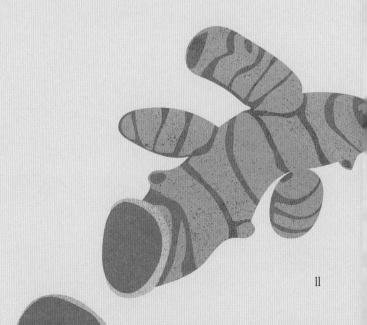

# Spicy (or Pungent)

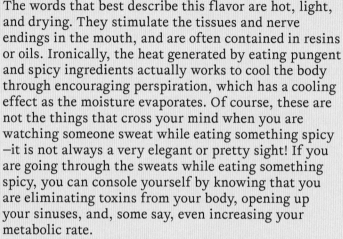

The words that best describe this flavor are hot, light, and drying. They stimulate the tissues and nerve endings in the mouth, and are often contained in resins or oils. Ironically, the heat generated by eating pungent and spicy ingredients actually works to cool the body through encouraging perspiration, which has a cooling effect as the moisture evaporates. Of course, these are not the things that cross your mind when you are watching someone sweat while eating something spicy —it is not always a very elegant or pretty sight! If you are going through the sweats while eating something spicy, you can console yourself by knowing that you are eliminating toxins from your body, opening up your sinuses, and, some say, even increasing your metabolic rate.

A popular myth is that spicy food aggravates the stomach and causes indigestion. Badly balanced flavors can have this effect. All of the recipes in this book balance pungency and spice with other flavors. I always tell my team when I start to train them to cook my family recipes, that if the only flavor a person can taste from a dish is chiles and heat, it is an indication that the cook failed to balance the flavors. The role of the conductor of an orchestra is to give each instrument enough importance—the same applies to the cook when balancing flavors!

Nigella seeds and mustard seeds are excellent for adding depth and complexity to otherwise simple dishes, while mustard oil brings a distinctive, bold flavor. The careful use of chiles can elevate your dishes by stimulating the palate and encouraging salivation, which helps the flavors build and linger on the tongue. When used thoughtfully, chiles don't just add heat—they enhance the overall taste experience, allowing the other ingredients to shine. It's not about overwhelming the senses with spice but using it as a tool to bring balance, allowing each element of the dish to play its part in harmony.

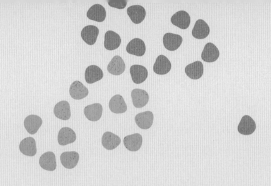

# Sweet

In Indian cuisine, sweet flavors are not limited to the more obvious ingredients like ghee, sugar, or honey. One of the less intuitive but fascinating aspects of the Indian understanding of taste—especially in the context of Ayurveda—is that rice, along with other staples like eggs and red lentils, are considered to have a naturally sweet flavor. The "sweet" flavor, or *madhura rasa* in Ayurveda, refers not just to sugary sweetness but also to ingredients that have a calming, cooling effect on the body and mind.

Rice, a staple in many Indian households, is classified as sweet because it nourishes, soothes, and provides energy. Its mild, neutral taste becomes more apparent when paired with spiced curries or dal, allowing the natural sweetness to balance the heat and pungency of the meal. Rice is also considered grounding and balancing in Ayurveda, promoting strength and vitality. Its cooling properties are especially valued in warmer climates, where foods that calm the digestive system and cool the body are essential for maintaining health.

In the broader culinary landscape, sweet flavors are integral to balancing the six tastes recognized in Ayurvedic tradition. In this context, sweet foods like rice are seen as nourishing and rejuvenating, which is why they are central to Indian meals. Sweetness is the taste associated with contentment, satisfaction, and comfort, and rice, being filling and soothing, embodies these qualities.

While some regional cuisines, like that of Gujarat, emphasize sweet elements in main courses, the subtle sweetness of rice plays an important balancing role across many Indian dishes. Even in savory meals, this natural sweetness helps harmonize the meal, making it not only delicious but also nutritionally balanced. In my own home, meals would often start with savory dishes, but there was always a place for sweet elements, whether it was the rice on the plate or the promise of dessert, something my father always made sure to ask about before diving into his meal!

# Salty (or Umami)

The flavor of umami or salt is an important element in any meal. It enhances the overall taste of the meal. Salt stimulates the salivary glands and enables digestion and absorption of food. Over the sultry, humid monsoon months in Calcutta, rock salt was always added to cut fruits and juices to replenish electrolytes that were lost through perspiration in the heat. I remember my mother making me drink a concoction of salt and sugar dissolved in water after I returned from a long day out in the sun, to help me rehydrate.

Salt is used not just to flavor food but also as an ingredient to purify and dehydrate food. In Bengal, before cooking any seafood, a mix of salt and turmeric is rubbed on the skin to clean it of impurities and bacteria. Bitter vegetables, such as *karela* (bitter gourd), are sprinkled with salt, which drains water from the vegetable and reduces its bitterness. Eggplants are also cut and covered with a sprinkling of salt to drain moisture, making the flesh less spongy, which helps it absorb less oil during cooking. Used in moderation, salt is an important part of our cuisine.

# Bitter

The word bitter is usually not associated with anything positive. From a bitter harvest to a bitter pill, we have strong negative connotations with this word. However, when it comes to cooking, bitter flavors can contribute hugely to our enjoyment of food and have many benefits to our bodies. Bitter foods often help cleanse the toxins in the body. Bitter vegetables, such as *karela* (bitter gourd), and spices like fenugreek seeds and cinnamon have long been associated with helping to regulate blood sugar.

Bitter foods have a sacred place in some regional cuisines. In Bengal, a ceremonial meal or wedding feast always begins with *Shukto* (see page 163), which is a traditional combination of vegetables, including bitter vegetables. The role of the dish is to stimulate the appetite and get the body ready to digest richer food by encouraging the secretion of digestive enzymes.

Sometimes, bitter flavors are not so obvious and are more subtle and layered, such as *kasuri methi* (dried fenugreek leaves) in butter chicken. The distinctive smoky and bitter flavor of the leaves balances the creamy buttery base of the chicken. Dark green leaves are also part of the bitter flavor profile, and they are always included in family meals when they are in season. For me, the highlight of winter in India has always been the abundance of local greens and spinach. Packed with vitamins and minerals, such as iron and vitamin A, many of these bitter foods boost immunity and strengthen resistance to disease.

# ESSENTIAL INGREDIENTS & COOKING TECHNIQUES

Despite my love for the artistry of Indian cooking, much of it is actually quite modular. To truly master these dishes, you need to understand the "why and how" behind preparing and combining the core elements. By learning these techniques and concepts, you'll gain the ability to cook almost any Indian dish with confidence.

It's not enough to just add spices or onions to a dish; to get the most out of these ingredients, you need to understand how to use them effectively. The best way to improve your cooking is by starting with what feels manageable—you don't have to perfect everything right away. Gradually internalize and apply these fundamentals over time. It's okay if you can't do everything perfectly, especially when time or ingredients are limited, but incorporating even some of these tips will make a massive difference. The aim of this book is to take you on a journey of flavors, and these techniques and methods are all ways in which you can add nuance to your cooking.

# Water in Indian cooking

It may seem rather strange to list water as an important ingredient in Indian cooking, but it is! Temperature control and proper use of water are vital components in good cooking.

Room-temperature water is needed to presoak chickpeas (garbanzo beans) and lentils, and to hydrate dough to make perfect rotis.

Sprays of cold water can stop vegetables from burning in hot pans and will allow them to gently steam while simultaneously deglazing the pan. They can also stop delicate powdered spices from scorching.

Warm water can be added to dishes to make a gravy or to protect tomato paste (tomato puree) from burning in hot, dry pans.

When boiling potatoes for Indian dishes, I always leave the skin on to prevent water from being absorbed into the potatoes (see page 95). If water enters the potatoes as they boil, they're more likely to break and fail to "seal" with a brown edge when added to hot oil and spices. Once potatoes that have been boiled in their skins are cool enough to touch, the skins can be removed. A word of warning: do not allow boiled potatoes to cool completely as the skins will then stick fast. If that happens, the only solution is to use a knife to take the potato skins off.

# Yogurt

A popular marinade for meats in the subcontinent, yogurt acts as a protective balm on meats to stop them from burning over high, direct heat. This is why many *kabab* recipes have yogurt in them. The yogurt not only acts as a tenderizer but as protection from the direct heat of broiling (grilling).

Always use full-fat yogurt when cooking or marinating, as it is the fat in the yogurt that can withstand the heat. Yogurt with a fat content any lower than 5 percent will split when heated, causing the product to break up into small balls of curds and whey. This is not just a visual issue—it will also make the base gravy taste bitter and you will lose the smoothness that full-fat yogurt brings to a dish. Always cook out the liquid released from yogurt, as the liquid will change the flavor of a dish.

# Ginger & garlic paste

Ginger and garlic are used extensively in this book, mostly as a paste to form the base of a gravy. I like to use two parts ginger to one part garlic. Avoid young ginger with pale, thin skin, as it will not have the depth of flavor needed for the dishes in this book. Fresh ginger is available in most supermarkets now and is also sold in Asian greengrocers. Please do not use ground ginger as an alternative (it lacks the depth of flavor of fresh ginger) or dried ginger powder (*sonth*), which has a very different flavor profile. Dried ginger powder is pungent and similar in flavor to dried mango powder, which is also tangy and pungent.

Combining ginger and garlic to make a paste is easier than making each paste individually. Once you have the requisite amount of peeled garlic and ginger ready, chop the garlic cloves roughly—even just cutting them in half can be adequate. Ginger requires more attention, as it is a fibrous root and can get stuck in the blades of a food processor or blender. Chop the ginger into quite small pieces so that it can be blended easily.

Add the chopped ginger and garlic to your food processor. It helps to have the minimum quantity required to cover the blade for most blenders or processors. If the paste looks dry and crumbly, add a splash of water and process the paste again. Ideally, you want the ginger and garlic paste to be smooth and amalgamated. Be careful when adding the water —start by adding a drip and then increase if required. If you add too much water, you will end up with a liquid with bits of ginger and garlic in it, and not a thick, blended paste. The perfect ginger and garlic paste should have the consistency of mustard or well-made custard.

If you make more paste than is required for your recipe, it can be stored in an airtight jar or container, where it will keep for up to a week. Do not use a wet spoon to take out the paste, as that will spoil it.

# Onions

In India, onions are not full of water and cook at a faster rate than many Western onions, which absorb more moisture from the soil. The first time I saw a large white onion, when I moved to Cambridge from Calcutta, it was such a shock! The other shock was learning how long it took to cook flabby white onion slices to crisp, dark brown, caramelized onion in hot oil.

There are some steps to make the onion frying process more enjoyable. First, decide what music or podcast you are going to listen to as you fry your onions—this is going to take time! Next is to start slicing the onions. You do not need to cut the onions as thin as your favorite social media influencer or chef on television—you just need to be consistent. All the slices need to be of equal thickness so that they all cook at the same rate. If you have uneven onion slices, the thinner slices will burn while the thicker slices will still be transparent and uncooked.

In all my recipes, I explain the cooking process of the onions. I want to give a couple of extra tips here:

The first tip is to add a generous pinch of salt to the onion slices once they have started cooking in the oil. This will pull out extra moisture and make the cooking process faster. The water being released from the onions will often be visible—it forms a white, frothy foam on the top of the frying onions. Eventually the froth settles down as the moisture evaporates from the pan.

The second tip is to add a generous pinch of white sugar on top of the frying onion slices—this helps add a deeper caramelized color and is a common practice in Bengal.

Finally, do not use a dull knife when slicing onions. The cleaner the slices of onion, the less the enzymes that sting your eyes and burn your hands will be released.

# Pickles

Pickled foods are an intrinsic part of South Asian culture. They can be sweet, sour, spicy, or any combination of these flavors, and are often found in Indian store-cupboards in sterilized jars of oil or vinegar. I remember watching jars of pickles rest for months and being told to shake them as a child. They can be made from a range of different ingredients—limes and raw mango tend to be the most common, but the method of pickling can be applied creatively to just about any fruit or vegetable.

The ready-made pickles you find in the "international section" of your favorite supermarket truly are the tip of the iceberg. I highly recommend making your own pickles at least once, as I believe it is a rite of passage for any serious home cook! Remember, a long fermenting process is not mandatory—"quick" or "instant" pickles exist too (see page 56).

# Chutneys

There are some basic principles in making a chutney. The first is to prepare the fruit or vegetable and ensure that no item has any pests or disease. It is important that all the pieces are cut to the same size—this ensures that all pieces taste the same, as they absorb the spices and flavors equally. The next step is to select the aromatics.

A well-made cooked chutney stimulates the palate from all angles. This layering of complex flavors begins with the introduction of aromatics in oil, followed by pungent ingredients, like mustard, fennel, or dried chiles, to create a base of heat, spice, and aroma. These pungent flavors are often intensified by the addition of garlic and ginger, followed by a source of sweetness such as apples, tomatoes, or gooseberries. This sweetness is contrasted by a souring agent, such as tamarind or lemon. Cooked chutneys are often finished with sugar, which allows it to become thick and sticky when cooked down with all the other ingredients. Cooking down chutneys amalgamates all the layers of flavor and preserves the chutney by removing most of the moisture. With the right precautions (e.g., using dry silverware to handle chutney and sterilized jars), cooked chutneys can last for months in the refrigerator.

Raw chutneys, made with fresh, raw ingredients, are prepared on an ad hoc basis and are meant to be eaten fresh with each meal rather than stored for extended periods. These chutneys vary widely in flavor and content, but are often made with green chiles, garlic, and herbs, and were traditionally prepared on *batan*-style grinding stones to produce a unique and rustic flavor and texture. Using an implement like this, or another natural stone vessel, such as a *molcajete*, is the best way to achieve a truly authentic fresh chutney, but a blender will also work fine!

# Hari Chatni

SERVES 4–6
TANGY – LEMON

3½oz (100g) cilantro leaves
    and stems
1¾oz (50g) fresh mint
2 green chiles, finely chopped
juice of ½ lemon
2 tsp white sugar
1in (2.5cm) piece of fresh root
    ginger, peeled and grated
4 tbsp water
½ tsp salt

Every household has its own recipe for cilantro and green chile chutney. In monsoon season, fresh chiles are less spicy, so the addition of ginger gives the chutney an added sharpness to compensate. For many years, this kind of chutney was made at home by grinding the fresh ingredients on a *sil batta* (or *shil nora* in Bengali). This grinder consisted of two parts: a flat stone base and a cylindrical or small stone, which was used to crush the fresh ingredients laid out on the flat stone. Chutneys made this way are always smooth and thick, as very little water is needed to crush the ingredients. Today, almost every household uses a blender or food processor to make the chutney.

Do not use bird's eye chiles for this chutney, as they will be too spicy. Larger chiles generally tend to be less spicy. You should always adjust a chutney to your taste, there are no hard and fast rules. The salt, sugar, and lemon content can all be varied here to get the chutney to your taste.

Wash the cilantro and chop finely, including the stems. Wash the mint and pull the leaves from the stalks. Add all the ingredients to a food processor and blend. You may need to stop to push down the leaves from time to time. The chutney should be smooth in texture without any visible leaves.

# Dhania Pudina Chutney

MAKES 20 SERVINGS
SWEET – COCONUT

⅓ cup (100ml) coconut
    milk *optional*
2½ cups (50g) fresh mint leaves
1 fresh green chile, chopped
½ tsp sugar
salt, to taste

There are two versions of this mint and green chile chutney. A thicker one made without coconut milk pairs well with dishes such as the Tawa Toastie (page 106), while a creamier one with coconut milk pairs better with dishes such as the Aloo Makai Tikki (page 65). After making this chutney a couple of times, you will gain an understanding of where and when the mild sweetness and creamy texture of coconut milk will be a valuable addition.

Combine all the ingredients in a food processor and blend until smooth. Taste and adjust the seasoning as needed.

# Cooking
# with spices

## POWDERED SPICES

Cooking spices to maximize their aroma, flavor, and
color is a very important part of Indian culinary tradition.
The taste of raw or burned spices cannot be camouflaged
in a dish. Powdered spices are usually added when there
are already onions/ginger/garlic and other ingredients
in the pot. If you add powdered spices directly to hot oil
where there are no other ingredients, be prepared to be quick
to add the next ingredient or sprays of water to reduce the
temperature and prevent the powdered spice from burning.
Most of the recipes in this book have the powdered spices
added after other ingredients. The powdered spices
then need to be cooked out, usually with the addition
of other ingredients and some liquid, which could be water,
yogurt, or tomatoes. This process of cooking out is known as
*bhuno*—cooking your powdered spices in a buffer of oil until
the excess liquid has evaporated is crucial in achieving
an aromatic, smoky flavor that infuses into the entire dish.
Once you see oil come to the edges of your spices, you
can be fairly confident that all excess liquid has evaporated.
This lets you know that you no longer need to *bhuno* your
spices and can focus on ensuring your spice paste does not
get stuck and/or burned in the pan.

## WHOLE SPICES

These are used as aromatics and are usually added
at the beginning of the recipe. Again, like powdered
garam masala (see page 32), do not buy large bags
of whole cardamom pods or other whole spices. Although
their shelf life is much longer, it is always better to buy
a smaller quantity of spices and replace them more
frequently. This will ensure that the spice will not
deteriorate over time and that the oils within the spice
will be of optimum quality. You need to store the spices
away from direct sunlight and in airtight containers.
Store all the spices separately so their aromas do not
mix (although I usually store mace and nutmeg together
as they are both from the same plant). Dried whole red
chiles should be stored in a roomy container. If you force
the chiles into a small storage container, they are more
likely to break and you will soon see a settlement of chile
seeds at the bottom as they fall out of the broken chiles.

## WHOLE DRIED RED CHILES

I prefer to use whole dried red chiles instead of chili powder. Infusing chiles into hot oil adds a spicy flavor to the oil, which both coats and infuses with the ingredients in the pot–this is a more diffused and subtle way to flavor a dish with chiles. An advantage of using this method over using chili powder is that you do not need to digest chili powder and your lips will not burn if you are sensitive to chiles. With experience, you will come to know which dried whole chiles are spicier. The basic rule of thumb is that the smaller a chile, fresh or dried, the spicier it will be. The larger, crinkly, whole Kashmiri chile is like sweet paprika, adding only a little heat, while some of the cherrylike, small dried red chiles from South India have a lot of fire power. Treat the latter with a lot of respect–do not pierce or break them, as it will release the seeds and hot chemicals from the membrane into your dish. If you love chiles, you can look for these hotter chiles in South Asian supermarkets. Use them especially for tempering dal.

# Roasting spices

Heating and crushing certain whole spices and seeds adds a layer of aroma and flavor to a dish that no store-bought, packaged ground spice can. Heating spices can also bring healing properties to a dish. (A good example is clove oil, which contains eugenol. Clove oil has been attributed with antioxidant properties and for centuries was used in India for pain relief, especially for toothache.) Cooking to maximize the benefits of all ingredients goes back to our ancient culinary heritage, where food was seen as medicinal. I am a great believer in mindful cooking, understanding the value each ingredient brings to a dish and, most importantly, recognizing that the most invaluable of all ingredients is your time, your touch, your sensibilities, and emotion as you cook.

The fragrance of freshly ground spices is hard to describe. The closest thing I could compare it to is the heady aroma of crushed *gulab* petals (the dark, velvety Indian rose) or the earthy aroma released from the forest floor as you walk on it. It must be experienced to understand it. Roasting and grinding spices as you cook may sound like a lot of additional work when an alternative is available in a convenient form, but the difference freshly roasted spices make to a dish is significant–they elevate the complex flavors of a dish to a higher level. Many spices, such as cassia bark, cumin, nutmeg, and cardamom, contain oils–it is heat from roasting or frying the spices that releases this oil. Adding whole spices in hot oil to temper dal (see page 127) is one way to release the aroma and oils of spices. The other way is to roast and grind them.

In this section I list two of the most essential spices that I grind at home–cumin seeds and garam masala (a spice mixture). But do note: not every spice has to be freshly roasted and ground. Store-bought ground turmeric works well and ground coriander can be used in a pinch. (See more about powdered spices on page 26.)

## HOME-ROASTED CUMIN SEEDS

Roasting and grinding cumin seeds transforms the tiny gray spice into a light brown, earthy–flavored powder. To get the full benefit of the spice flavor and aroma it must be crushed or ground soon after it has been roasted. One tip to ensure that you do not burn the spice while roasting is to place some unroasted cumin seeds on a light-colored plate next to the pan where you will be roasting them. The change of color as you roast the spices is very subtle–if you do not have the unroasted spices to compare against, you run a high risk of burning the small cumin seeds as you roast them. Once the seeds are burned, they will take on an unpleasant, bitter flavor and must be discarded. There is no saving burned spices.

Before roasting the cumin seeds, place a wide empty plate on the work surface nearby. You will transfer the roasted seeds to this. It is important that the seeds are not piled in a bowl or transferred to a small plate after roasting, as they need space to cool down quickly (the spice will continue to cook with the residual heat even after you remove it from the pan).

Ideally, use a cast-iron skillet to roast spices, as the heat on the base of the pan will be evenly diffused. The other alternative is to use a heavy-based frying pan.

Start by measuring out the quantity of cumin seeds you want to roast. Heat the skillet or frying pan over a medium-low heat. When the pan is hot, pour in the cumin seeds and use a spoon to immediately stir. You can shake the pan instead of using a spoon, but I feel a spoon does a better job! Ideally, the seeds should be in a single layer to ensure that they roast evenly, and there should be space to constantly move the seeds, so one side does not get over-roasted. Roast the seeds for around 2 minutes. If they start to smoke and turn dark very quickly, the pan is too hot. The roasting needs to be slow and gentle, so that the heat from the pan penetrates to the inside of the seed and does not just burn the surface. There are two things to look out for when roasting cumin seeds: The first is a visual comparison with unroasted cumin seeds. The seeds in the pan should darken by a few shades in comparison to the unroasted seeds. The second is the aroma. The seeds should start to emit a beautiful, nutty aroma. When the seeds look ready, transfer them to a plate and spread them out. Do not transfer to paper towels—you need the oils that have been released by the roasting to stay inside the spice and not be absorbed by paper.

The cooled seeds should be crushed immediately in a pestle and mortar or in a spice grinder. I prefer to use a spice grinder, as the cumin powder comes out smooth. If you have any extra, it can kept in an airtight spice jar. However, use it up soon, as the ground cumin will lose its smoky aroma over time. Ideally, you should aim to consume the powder within a month, but it can still be used for 3–4 months afterward.

# HOME-ROASTED GARAM MASALA

The name of this spice mix is a bit of a misnomer–*garam* means "hot" in Hindi and *masala* means "a spice mix" or "mixture." Garam masala is not hot as in the chile heat you could expect from a hot sauce. Instead, it is hot as in strongly fragrant, woody, and warming. The mix of spices in a garam masala brings heat to the body and energizes it.

The core spices of garam masala (cassia bark, clove, cardamom, and bay leaf) can be added whole at the start of a recipe to infuse the oil/ghee in the hot pan with the warming fragrance of the spices. But powdered garam masala is often added toward the end of cooking–this helps retain the aroma of the spices so that they don't lose their fragrance during the cooking process. You will find both methods used throughout this book.

My goal when writing this cookbook was to inspire you to embark on a journey of exploration in Indian cooking and to look for other recipes to further expand your horizons. Other recipes for Indian dishes may have you adding a store-bought garam masala, so I wanted to include a basic garam masala recipe that will allow you to stick to new recipes, while elevating their flavor with a homemade spice blend. Some commercially produced garam masalas can have up to 12 different spices, and most manufacturers do not give a breakdown of the proportion of each individual spice used. It is safe to assume that the bulk of the spices will be the cheaper "filler" spices, and not the more expensive spices like cardamom and cloves. A jar of ready-made garam masala may seem to be a cheap and convenient purchase, but it is not going to lift your cooking in the same way that freshly ground and roasted garam masala will. On the following page are a couple of variations of the mixture.

# Garam masala

**BENGALI GARAM MASALA**
*(this is the one made at my home in Calcutta with just a handful of spices)*

20 green cardamom pods
1 tbsp cloves
3 x 3-in (7.5-cm) cinnamon sticks *I use cinnamon as cassia bark is more robust and fiery, and Bengali dishes tend to be more delicate and fragrant*
3 Indian bay leaves (cassia leaves) *if small, use 4 or 5*

**NORTH INDIAN GARAM MASALA**
*(this was the combination used in my paternal family)*

2 mace blades
1 tbsp cloves
¼oz (10g) black peppercorns
2 x 2-in (5-cm) pieces of cassia bark
¼oz (10g) green cardamom pods
¾oz (20g) cumin seeds
½oz (15g) coriander seeds
¼ nutmeg, crumbled
1 large Indian bay leaf (cassia leaf)

**OPTIONAL ADDITIONS TO NORTH INDIAN MIX**

different kinds of peppercorns: white or green
2 seeds that are good for digestion: 1 tbsp fennel seeds and/or 1 tbsp ajwain (carom seeds)

Do not bruise or break any of the spices before roasting them—cardamom seeds will burn, and broken pieces of bay leaf will become brittle. Keep a plate ready nearby to transfer the whole spices to when roasted.

Heat a cast-iron skillet or heavy-based frying pan over a low-medium heat. When hot, add all the whole spices (except the bay leaf, which should only be added toward the end) and stir gently to ensure they are evenly heated. It will take 12–15 minutes to roast them completely. If the spices are smoking too quickly, reduce the heat or take the pan off the heat briefly to prevent the spices from burning. In the last few minutes, add the bay leaf and let it darken. Transfer all the spices to the waiting plate, spread out and leave to cool.

As some of the spices are hard, I recommend a spice grinder to grind the masala. Do not try to grind the spices while they are still warm—the masala will become oily in the grinder and stop rotating, and the larger pieces of cinnamon and cassia bark will get jammed in the blades. Once the spices are cooled, break the cinnamon and cassia bark into smaller pieces and tear the bay leaf into smaller pieces too. I have seen my aunts hit the cardamom pods with the end of a rolling pin to crack them open, but I only do that if I am roasting and grinding black cardamom, as the outer cover of black cardamom is much harder than green cardamom. You can add the cardamom whole to the grinder. Start by grinding the masala in very short spurts—this is necessary to break down the harder and bigger pieces in the mix. Shake the grinder and continue in short spurts until you can see that the pieces of spice are smaller. At this point you can grind on full power. You may end up with some hard pieces while most of the garam masala has become powder. I usually pick them out and add them directly to the cooking pot or keep them to add to my next *pulao*. The garam masala should be stored immediately in an airtight container to preserve the aroma. Stored in a cool, dry place, it will keep for up to 2 months.

# Cooking with ghee

Sweet, aromatic ghee, golden in color with nutty undertones of flavor, is a joy to cook with. Store-bought ghee is a pale shadow of ghee made at home. A word of warning: making ghee may become your new obsession once you realize how easy it is to do and how delicious it is! My paternal family moved from their ancestral lands in Bulandshahr and settled in Aligarh, a city famous for two things: white butter and locks. As a child, I remembered watching the butter being churned in the courtyard in a terra-cotta pot using a stick wrapped with a thick rope. The churning noise was so rhythmic—the rope and stick swishing the cream like a paddle until the fat separated from the liquid. We would spread dollops of that white butter on chapati and paratha. The white butter was then used to make ghee. I only realized that the home-churned white butter was made into ghee when I was much older, in my late teens. Somehow, they looked too different to me to have any connection. When I told my mother that, she laughed and told me ghee had a secret life—it transformed itself from butter to a beautiful golden liquid just like a caterpillar into a butterfly!

## WHY USE GHEE

The nutty and sweet undertones of ghee is a big reason to use it when cooking—it will add a distinct fragrance and flavor that will add an extra layer of complexity to your dishes. Ghee has a far higher smoke point than butter (due to the removal of milk solids that are prone to burning) and a comparable smoke point to traditional "frying" oils, like sunflower oil. This makes it incredibly versatile. The removal of milk solids all but removes the lactose sugars from the butter too. This makes it suitable for many people who are lactose intolerant. Ghee does not need to be stored in the refrigerator and if it solidifies due to cooler weather, it will rapidly melt once heated. Ghee keeps well and if properly stored will not go rancid for a very long time. Small earthenware or glass jars of homemade ghee make wonderful gifts for friends and family.

# How to make ghee

There are three steps to making ghee:
1. Collecting the cream from the milk.
2. Churning the milk cream to make butter.
3. Clarifying the butter to make ghee.

There is also the jump-start method, too, where you can skip the first two steps and make the ghee with good quality, store-bought, preferably organic unsalted butter. This one-step method makes the entire process of making ghee much faster. However, the ghee will not have the same intensity of flavor, as the flavor of commercial butter is more muted.

I list the full process below for the day when you decide to step off the fast track and into the slow lane to make ghee from scratch. Your reward will be a jar of golden goodness that you can add to all your future dishes.

## STEP 1 (THE OLD-FASHIONED WAY)

The quality of your milk is very important if you want to make ghee from scratch. The layer of *malai*, or cream, on the top of the milk that was used to make ghee was usually collected from buffalo milk in most households I knew in India. Just as quality mozzarella is often made with buffalo milk because it has a higher fat content than cows' milk, the same applies to the milk for ghee.

To collect cream, the milk cannot be homogenized. All the fat from the milk needs to be separated and that cannot happen with milk where the fat has been blended into the milk. In the old-fashioned way, the cream would be collected over a few days and stored. This was mainly for logistical reasons, as there was limited or no refrigeration, the daily milk that was delivered to the house would be unpasteurized, and each household would often boil the milk before consumption. Even in a very urban setting in Calcutta, we often had the *gwala* (milkman) come to our house with the cow and milk it outside our gate to deliver fresh milk daily. That fresh milk was then boiled and cooled. The cooling process resulted in the cream forming a skin on the top of the milk, which would be skimmed off and stored to make butter. As we had a household of very sly home cats in Calcutta who often ganged up with feral cats from outside to raid the kitchen, we had to tightly tie a muslin cloth with several knots on top of the milk pan to save it from the cat gang.

The cream layer from the milk would usually be collected for a week before it was made into butter. This cream-storage process would trigger a change in the culture of the cream, adding another subtle layer of flavor. This is how ghee was traditionally made, but unfortunately, food safety standards mean that the process is no longer considered safe. A recipe I recommend for making ghee is below.

## STEP 1   (THE EASIER WAY)

If you can get good-quality thick cream where you live, you do not have to go through this protracted cream-collection process. The cream will not have the cultured transformation, but you save on time and effort, which is the more practical way to make butter. Unlike the old-fashioned collection of cream, where the liquid that separated from the fat was often a bit bitter because of the culture transformation, the buttermilk/water that separates after churning fresh cream is sweeter, and can be added to soups or muffin/bread doughs.

## STEP 2

I am not going to suggest the pot and rope paddle churning process! There are gadgets available to churn butter, which you can buy online, but the most efficient is a food processor fitted with a metal blade. The cream cannot be too cold or too hot—you need to take the cream out of the refrigerator and let it come to about 54–59°F (12–15°C). If you do not have a thermometer, your cream should be slightly below room temperature.

Churn the cream until it starts to form a thick consistency. Do not hesitate as you see it start to thicken—you must continue to churn until it separates into lumps of fat and a watery liquid. Once the cream has split, you have to consolidate and bring the fat together. Transfer the contents of the processor to a large glass bowl and add ice cubes and cold water. The fat will solidify and become compact.

Use your hands to separate the butter from the liquid and transfer to a clean work surface. Gently knead to extract any remaining liquid trapped inside the butter. Gently wash the butter with very cold water and press it to compact it, then transfer it to a clean container and refrigerate immediately.

This butter can be used right away if you want to use some before making ghee—I love adding crushed sea salt flakes and pepper to it before spreading on toast. Although

it is hard to be accurate, as a rough estimate, 4 cups (1 liter) of thick cream should yield at least 1 cup (500g) of butter.

## STEP 3

The process is the same, irrespective of quantity, but starting with 1–1½ cups (500–750g) of butter is good initially. 1 cup (500g) of butter will yield almost 2 cups (500ml) of ghee. With increased experience, you can make larger quantities.

To prevent any burns from the hot butter, cook in a deep, heavy-based pan, such as a stockpot, with a safe margin of space to avoid spluttering. Add the butter to your pan, then heat over a medium-low heat until it melts. Once all the butter has melted, increase the heat to bring it to boiling point—the moisture in the butter will start to come to the surface as white foam. Use a slotted metal spoon to skim it off, and discard it. Reduce the heat to low and continue to simmer uncovered. While the foam comes to the surface, you will see milk solids settling at the bottom of the pan. Do not stir and disturb the milk solids—they will slowly change color, from creamy white to brown. The ghee should now be a glistening, light golden color. Turn the heat off. When the ghee has cooled a little, strain it through a muslin or fine cheesecloth into a clean glass or earthenware jar. The milk solids can be crumbled and used when cooking rice or vegetables, or added to lentils. The milk solids should be a deep brown and should not be burned. Do not use if burned.

Ghee will keep unrefrigerated for months, but the usual precautions apply—do not put a wet spoon into the ghee jar. Pour the ghee from the jar even if your ladle is clean and dry. Minimizing the risk of adding foreign microbes or bacteria to the ghee will keep it safe for months.

## FLAVORED GHEE

Plain ghee is, of course, more versatile—flavoring it with a spice could limit your options, but it is definitely worth thinking about once you become a seasoned ghee maker. When the butter is melted, you can add a tablespoon of spice tied in a muslin pouch, and let it cook with the ghee, infusing with spice while slowly simmering. Remove the spice pouch, and discard it when the ghee is ready to be strained. I suggest sticking to one spice only. A great option is fenugreek seeds, which have medicinal properties for balancing blood sugar. Fenugreek seeds are bitter, and by infusing them in ghee you can add them to your food and not have a strong bitter flavor in the dish. Other spices you can use are cloves, cinnamon sticks, and dried red chiles.

# Other cooking oils

When it comes to cooking fats in Indian cooking, not all fats/oils are the same! As my mother is from Bengal, I start with the often misunderstood mustard oil.

## MUSTARD OIL

Mustard oil has been used in Bengal for generations to prepare the region's pungent dishes. It is a great oil to cook with due to its high smoke point, which makes it a versatile ingredient that features in a range of recipes. To get the most out of mustard oil, remove its bitterness by first heating the oil to its smoking point. Once the oil's smoke point is reached, you must reduce the heat and allow the oil to come to an appropriate cooking temperature. This is also the point where you can add another oil to the pan (see Pineapple Pachadi, page 235). This will further help to reduce the temperature of the mustard oil from its smoking point. My favorite way to use mustard oil is in dishes like Tehari (see page 213), where the complex flavors of the oil are infused throughout the rice.

## COCONUT OIL

This is more commonly used in South India, where there is an abundance of coconut trees. It was not an oil that was used a lot in my home when I lived in India, but in some regions this is the most common cooking fat. Coconut oil is a good alternative to ghee if you are looking for a vegan option. Virgin cold-pressed coconut oil has a slightly lower smoking point than refined coconut oil, but both versions of the oil are close to ghee in their smoking point, which means they can both be safely used for deep-frying and tempering spices. If you anticipate reaching very high cooking temperatures (above 350°F/180°C), use refined coconut oil.

## NEUTRAL VEGETABLE OILS

These are refined oils, such as sunflower, rapeseed (canola), grapeseed, and corn oil. Cold-pressed versions of these oils are also available, but the commercially available oils are usually processed and tend to be colorless and without any flavor. In India, peanut (groundnut) oil was very popular before vegetable oil took over in the 1980s. Packaged and sold as a "healthier" oil, sunflower oil was presented as an alternative that contained fewer saturated fats compared to the then market leader Dalda.

The advantage of these oils is their high smoking point, which is especially suitable for many of the recipes in this book, where the spices, onions, and ginger/garlic paste are cooked over a medium-high heat for prolonged periods of time. The other advantage of using a neutral vegetable oil is that it will not clash with the infusion of spices, seeds, and chiles. The oil will soak up all these flavors and subsequently impart them into your other ingredients. This helps to layer flavors as you cook and means you do not need to worry about the flavor of your oil clashing with the rest of your ingredients.

# Rice

Rice holds a sacred place in Indian culture (see also page 13). When a child is ready to be weaned, a formal rice ceremony is performed, attended by the family's elders. In this ritual, called *mukhēbhāt* where I am from in West Bengal, or more commonly *annaprasana* or "grain initiation" in Sanskrit, an elder places cooked rice into the child's mouth, marking their introduction to solid food. Clearly, rice is more than just a grain—it is spiritually and culturally intertwined with the Indian palate, cuisine, and heritage.

When I was very young, I remember my mother telling me that every grain of rice had my name on it–that it was part of my *kismet*, my destiny, to receive that rice. I recall in my childhood being served rice, with each spoonful on my plate always followed by a little extra. These small rituals around rice have stayed with me. Even now, when I serve food and someone asks for just one spoonful of rice, I can't bring myself to not chase with a few more grains in a second spoon.

# How to cook rice

SERVES 4–5
SWEET – RICE

Other than using a rice cooker, this is probably the easiest way to consistently make perfectly cooked rice. I always recommend making more than you need, because the rice will keep well for a day or two and can be used in dishes like fried rice. Always use a 2:1 ratio of water to rice, and if reheating ensure that the rice is reheated until it's piping hot.

## ABSORPTION METHOD

1 cup (200g) basmati rice
2 cups (500ml) water
1½ tsp salt

Spread your rice out on a tray and check for any impurities, then put the dry rice in a large bowl. Pour enough water to cover well (at least 2 cups) into the bowl from a measuring cup (this avoids breaking the grains with the pressure you would get from your kitchen tap). Wash the rice gently by swirling it in one direction with your hand. Swirling in both directions can cause the grains to bang into each other and break, and this will ruin the texture of your rice. Drain, then continue this washing process with fresh water until the water runs clear. Cover the rice with fresh water and leave to soak for 30 minutes–1 hour, then drain again.

Transfer the rice to a pan that has a lid. Boil the measured water to cook your rice in a kettle. Add the boiling water to your rice, turn the heat to high and gently stir once or twice as the rice begins to boil. When it's boiling, add the salt and stir, then cover the pan with the lid and reduce to a simmer for 10–15 minutes.

After this time, check to see if all the water has been absorbed, and cook for a little longer if it has not. Once all the water has been absorbed, stir the rice once more, cover the pan with a clean kitchen cloth, and leave undisturbed for 10 minutes.

Use a fork to gently separate the grains and fluff up the rice before serving.

## DRAINING METHOD

1 cup (200g) basmati rice
2 cups (500ml) water
1½ tsp salt

Wash the rice as described above.

Drain the washed rice in a colander and spread out on paper towels to remove excess water.

Bring your measured water to a rolling boil in a saucepan and add the salt, followed by the rice. Cook over a high heat, stirring a few times in the same direction. After 5 minutes have passed, check that the rice is almost ready—do not be tempted to wait until it is very soft as residual heat will continue to cook the rice. Remove a grain and squeeze it to test—the rice is done when the grain is cooked through but still firm. It should become a paste when squeezed, but the center should still be al dente. This can take up to 10 minutes depending on the pot and the rice.

Drain in a colander over the sink. Let the rice rest, covered, for 2–3 minutes before serving. Fluff up the rice with a fork before serving to separate the grains.

# The importance of heat

A very important element in getting the most out of ingredients, especially spices, is temperature control while roasting and frying. Many spices contain oils that can be extracted through dry-roasting. These oils bring pungency and smokiness that can elevate your cooking dramatically. It is a challenge not to burn spices when dry-roasting, but starting off with very small quantities and keeping the temperature low will minimize the risk of burning, and allow the pan to heat evenly. The ideal surface on which spices should be roasted is cast iron, but any surface that can heat evenly and hold a constant temperature will work.

When frying spices, the pan should be on a medium-high heat. Once whole spices have been added to hot oil, it is a race against time to prevent them from burning. It is therefore vital to have your prepared ingredients nearby so they can quickly be added to the pan to drop the temperature of the oil enough to stop your spices from burning.

Preheating the oil when frying any ingredient is essential, as the oil temperature will fall with the addition of room-temperature or refrigerated ingredients. It is important not to crowd the pan and to fry your food in batches. This is especially true for breaded and battered recipes, as if the oil gets cold, these become greasy and soggy. Besides using a quick-read thermometer (which I never use), I recommend adding a piece of bread or the tip of an onion to the hot oil, to check that your oil is up to temperature. When deep-frying, don't hesitate to check the oil between batches. It's vital to ensure that you do not attempt to cook in cold oil.

Generally speaking, apart from mustard oil, avoid heating oils past their smoking point, as this will lead to an unpleasant flavor.

গ্রীষ্ম

◇ 1 ◇

# GRISHSHO

Summer

Summer brings golden days full
of sunshine and the sweet nostalgia
of mango season from my childhood.
It's a time for unhurried meals and long,
leisurely conversations around the table,
basking in the warmth of the day and the
company of loved ones. With longer days
and shorter nights, summer invites us
to slow down, enjoy the moment, and
make the most of the light.

In these intensely hot months, lighter
dishes come to the forefront, offering a
refreshing balance to the heat. Recipes such
as Matira Curry (page 52), Chotpoti (page
76), and Dahi Vada (page 78) truly shine in
the summer, with their vibrant flavors and
cooling qualities. These dishes, perfect for a
relaxed afternoon or evening meal, capture
the essence of summer—simple, light, and
deeply satisfying. Whether you're dining
with friends or family, summer is the
season to linger at the table and
savor the golden moments.

# Shimla Mirch Paneer Tarkari

### BELL PEPPERS WITH CRUMBLED PANEER

Named after Shimla, the winter capital of the British Empire in India, *shimla mirchi* (or capsicums/bell peppers, as they were called in English) were introduced by the British to India. Initially grown in South and Central America, the vegetable made its way to Europe through the travels of Christopher Columbus. The British then brought the seeds of bell peppers to India and grew them in the cooler climate up in the mountains. Often added to bring a dash of color and texture to a dish (vitamin C, too!), here I have combined them with paneer.

5 tbsp vegetable oil

1 tsp black mustard seeds

2 dried red chiles

5 garlic cloves, roughly chopped

2¾lb (1.2kg) bell peppers of different colors (to suit your preference), washed, cored, seeds removed, and cut into 1½in (4cm) squares

1 tsp ground turmeric

1 tsp chili powder

1½ tsp salt

1lb 2oz (500g) paneer, roughly crumbled *an interesting swap is chopped hard-boiled eggs or canned sweet corn*

1 tbsp lemon juice

2 tbsp chopped cilantro, to garnish

**FOR THE ROASTED SPICE MIX**

1 tsp cumin seeds

2 tsp coriander seeds

1-in (2.5-cm) cinnamon stick, broken into small pieces

4 whole cloves

8 peppercorns

2 green cardamom pods, lightly crushed

Heat a dry cast-iron skillet over a low to medium heat. Add all the ingredients for the roasted spice mix to the pan and keep stirring to ensure they all roast evenly, about 3–5 minutes. All the spices will darken a couple of shades and some of the oil-based spices, like the cloves, will release a distinctive, smoky aroma. Transfer the roasted spices to a plate and spread them out so they cool down faster.

Once cool, transfer the spices to a grinder and pulse in short bursts to help break down the cinnamon and cardamom. The aim is to get a rough powder. If there are stubborn bits of cinnamon or cardamom that are not powdered, discard them.

Warm the oil in a *karai* or wok over a medium heat until it is shimmering. Add the mustard seeds and wait for them to pop, then add the whole dried chiles followed by the garlic. Stir until the garlic is tinged brown at the edges. Add all the cubes of bell pepper and continue to stir-fry for a couple of minutes. Add the turmeric, chili powder, and salt, and stir-fry for a few more minutes. Add 1 teaspoon of the ground roasted spice mix and keep stirring. When the edges of the pepper cubes start to curl (the pepper should still be a bit crunchy), add the crumbled paneer (or chopped eggs/sweet corn) and stir for a couple more minutes so that the paneer is evenly distributed. Add the lemon juice and stir well.

Taste for seasoning, garnish with the chopped cilantro, and serve. If you are making this dish in advance, add the lemon juice and herbs after reheating the peppers.

# LIGHT SUMMER LUNCH

### Vegan-Friendly

This meal is a great way to use up leftover watermelon
or zucchini in your kitchen and is a great alternative to
putting together a rushed salad. This combination
requires minimal cooking time and maximizes your
opportunity to enjoy the sunshine (unless you live in the
UK, where summer sun is not guaranteed!). The layering
of spices and tangy *achar* pickle stimulates the palate. The
watermelon curry tastes good chilled, too,
so can work as an accompaniment to an omelette
or sandwich for another meal.

### MENU SUGGESTION

**Matira Curry**
*Sweet*
PAGE 52

**Zucchini Paratha**
*Bitter*
PAGE 53

**Gajar ka Achar**
*Tangy*
PAGE 56

# Matira Curry

RED WATERMELON CURRY

If you can add feta to watermelons and make a salad, you can add chiles and make this quintessentially Rajasthani dish. In an arid and parched land, the people living in the desert of Rajasthan found ways to survive the harsh summer months where very little vegetation grew. The *matira* curry was a clever way to use the one ingredient that was locally available in abundance—watermelon. My father's family originally came from Rajasthan and I remember my great grandmother telling me that the hotter the dry, scorching wind blew in the desert, the sweeter the watermelons got! The dish has a sweet and spicy flavor. It can be served as part of a barbecue menu and is a great accompaniment to any meal.

4 tbsp vegetable oil
½ tsp cumin seeds
4 dried whole chiles (medium heat), broken in half
1½-in (4-cm) fresh root ginger, peeled and finely grated
½ tsp ground turmeric
5½oz (150g) watermelon, peeled, juiced; plus 1lb 5oz–1lb 10oz (600–750g), cubed
1½ tsp salt
2 tsp sugar (any type)
4 tbsp lime juice
fresh mint, to garnish *optional*

Warm the oil in a *karai* or wok over a medium heat. Add the cumin seeds, then the broken chiles followed by the grated ginger and turmeric. Immediately add the watermelon juice and stir. Add the salt and sugar, then bring to a low rolling boil. When the juice has reduced by a third, add the watermelon cubes and cook for 4–5 minutes. Stir well, then taste and adjust the seasoning, adding lime juice for acidity.

If you like, you can serve the curry garnished with fresh mint (this would not have been available in summer in Rajasthan, but I like the combination of mint and watermelon).

*Pictured on pages 54–55*

# Zucchini Paratha

This is a beginner-friendly variation on traditional Indian stuffed parathas, which require patience and practice to perfect. Instead of creating a separate dough and stuffing, here the vegetables are minced and added to the flour to make up the dough. This method of incorporating the vegetable in the dough instead of stuffing it makes it much easier to roll, as stuffed parathas are prone to tearing and bursting during rolling and cooking.

5oz (150g) zucchini, finely chopped

¼ cup (50g) peas (if using frozen, thaw before use)

3 tbsp minced cilantro, leaves and stalks

½-in (1-cm) piece of fresh root ginger, peeled and minced

1 green chile, minced

½ tsp ground turmeric

1 tbsp toasted sesame seeds

3 tbsp ghee, melted (or vegetable oil)

1⅔ cups (200g) wholewheat or chapati flour

3¼ cups (100g) plain flour, plus extra for dusting

1 tsp salt

4 tbsp full-fat plain yogurt (or nondairy alternative)

In a food processor, blitz together the zucchini, peas, fresh cilantro, ginger, chile, turmeric, sesame seeds, and 2 tablespoons of the ghee (or oil).

Sift together the two flours and salt, then add to the food processor a little at a time, blitzing after each addition. Halfway through adding the flour, add the yogurt and continue to blend. You need to end up with a soft and pliant dough—it should not be sticky. Depending on the amount of liquid released from the zucchini, you may need to add a little water or more flour to get the dough to the right consistency. Transfer the dough to a flour-dusted work surface and knead with your knuckles until it is soft enough that you can make a thumb imprint on the dough. Cover and leave to rise in a cool place for 1 hour.

Divide the dough into 6 equal parts and roll each part into a ball, ensuring you keep them covered as you work. Using a rolling pin, roll out each ball to a 7-in (18-cm) circle. Do not be discouraged if your first few parathas are not perfect circles. Rolling perfect breads is a kitchen skill that is honed with time and practice—like flipping a pancake or making an omelette, there is a learning curve. The aim is to try to roll the bread evenly without making it so thin that it burns and dries out. It is better to prioritize getting an even thickness throughout rather than a perfectly round shape. Keep the rolled parathas covered.

Halfway through rolling the parathas, warm a *tawa* or flat griddle over a medium heat. When all the parathas are rolled, start cooking.

Place a paratha on the hot pan. When small bubbles start to appear, turn it over. After 30 seconds, lift one edge of the bread and drizzle ¼ teaspoon of the remaining ghee (or oil) on the pan. With a rolled-up piece of paper towel or a clean cloth, press the bread gently all around to ensure it is cooking evenly. Pay close attention to any signs of burning and reduce the heat, if necessary. Turn the bread again and add some more ghee (or oil), this time directly on the bread. Press down on the surface with a spatula. When the bread has brown speckles on it, remove to a plate. Wipe the pan before starting to cook the next bread.

The parathas can be cooked in advance and stored separated with parchment paper, then reheated in a dry pan over a low heat, but they are best enjoyed fresh off the *tawa*.

*Pictured on pages 54–55*

# Gajar ka Achar

PICKLED CARROTS WITH GARLIC AND CHILE

This recipe is a quick-cooked carrot oil pickle that does not require fermenting in a jar in the sunshine. This is a fast and efficient way to make pickle that is not weather-dependent. It also does not contain any vinegar, which may suit people who do not like the taste but want to enjoy the sour and tangy flavor of a pickle. The recipe can be halved if you would like to make a smaller quantity.

½ cup (120ml) mustard oil (or other vegetable oil)
2¼lb (1kg) carrots (any kind—black or heritage carrots are nice too)
1 tsp black mustard seeds
1 tsp yellow mustard seeds
½ tsp nigella seeds
1 tsp fennel seeds
20 curry leaves
6 dried red chiles
6 garlic cloves, thickly sliced
1 tbsp ground turmeric
1 tsp Kashmiri red chili powder
2 tsp salt
2 fresh green chiles, slit lengthways
4 tbsp lemon juice

If you are using mustard oil, it must be heated until smoking hot to get rid of the strong, pungent taste. Ensure you have your kitchen extractor fan on the highest setting and/or open your kitchen windows, if possible. Use a reliable, heavy-based, preferably cast-iron pan to heat the oil (a nonstick pan is likely to burn). Once the oil has reached smoking point, turn the heat off and leave the oil undisturbed on the stove to cool.

While the oil is cooling, peel the carrots and cut them into thin batons of about 2½in (6cm) long and ½in (1cm) wide (as long as the carrots are all cut to the same size, the actual size is not that important).

Once the carrots are ready to cook, set the pan of oil back over a medium heat. When the oil is heated, add the mustard seeds and wait until they make a popping sound before adding, in quick succession, the nigella seeds, fennel seeds, curry leaves, dried red chiles, and garlic. Stir until the garlic turns golden brown, then add the carrots, turmeric, chili powder, salt, and fresh green chiles, and continue to stir for 10 minutes. Turn off the heat, add the lemon juice, and gently mix in the pan.

Let the contents come to room temperature before transferring to a sterilized airtight jar and sealing tightly. Store in the fridge. It could be left out if the weather is cool, but the jar will need to be shaken every few days. (I know I should have an explanation on why you need to shake it—I don't! I just remember seeing the carrot pickle jars in my home being shaken every few days.) The pickle will be ready to consume in 24 hours.

*Pictured on pages 54–55*

# Achari Murgh

CHICKEN COOKED IN PICKLING SPICES AND YOGURT

This dish is a family favorite in my home in India. The use of pickling spices has been linked to the royal family of Bhopal, where some say the dish originated. The spices in this dish are the same as the combination of five seed spices that make up *panch phoran*, a mix that was heavily used in eastern India. Traditionally, *panch phoran* featured radhuni seeds (similar to celery seed), but they are hard to source outside Bengal. If you can source radhuni, use them to replace the black mustard seeds in the recipe below. You can also swap the chicken for red meat, if you prefer. You may need to tweak the seasoning and, of course, the cooking time. I prefer to cook this dish with chicken thighs on the bone as the bone adds flavor. If you want to make this dish with boneless chicken, please do not use chicken breast! Boneless chicken thighs will absorb the spices better and will not dry out.

6 tbsp vegetable oil

1 large onion, halved and sliced into thin half-moons

¼ tsp fennel seeds

¼ tsp black mustard seeds

¼ tsp nigella seeds

⅛ tsp fenugreek seeds

¼ tsp whole cumin seeds

1 tsp garlic paste

1 tbsp ginger paste

2¼lb (1kg) chicken thighs, bone-in, skin removed

½ tsp ground turmeric

1 tsp ground coriander

¼ tsp Kashmiri red chili powder

4 cups (1kg) plain yogurt

1 tsp salt, or to taste

1 fresh green chile, slit open lengthways; plus extra, chopped, to garnish

handful of cilantro leaves, chopped, to garnish

Heat the oil in a deep, heavy-based saucepan that has a lid, over a high heat. Take one tip of sliced onion and dip it into the edge of the oil. The oil is hot enough when the onion starts to sizzle immediately. If the onion does not sizzle immediately, wait for a minute and try with another slice of onion. Do not use the previous onion slice for the test, add that slice to the pan with the rest of the sliced onions when the oil is at temperature. Fry the onions until golden brown and caramelized, then remove with a slotted spoon, and spread over a plate so they don't become soggy.

To the same oil, add all the seed spices at the same time. Wait until you hear the mustard seeds pop, then add the garlic and ginger pastes, and stir until fragrant. If the paste is sticking to the pan, add a splash of water to deglaze the pan. Add the chicken thighs and brown the meat all over, then add the ground turmeric, coriander, and chili powder.

Crush the caramelized onions in a pestle and mortar (or in a bowl with the end of a rolling pin) and mix them with the yogurt, then add the mixture to the pan along with the salt, and bring to the boil. Cover the pan and reduce to a simmer for 30 minutes.

Remove the lid, add the slit chile, and continue to cook uncovered for a further 30 minutes, stirring the chicken until the sauce clings to the meat. Taste for seasoning and adjust if required. Garnish with chopped green chiles and cilantro, and serve with rice and salad.

# Chicken Jhal Farezi – From a Leftover Roast

The origin of this dish is fascinating. You can take the Brit out of Britain, but they will take the Sunday roast with them! In colonial times, the *khansama*, or head cook, of a British family in eastern India (modern-day Bangladesh and West Bengal) had to learn how to cook a traditional Sunday roast chicken, instructed by the *memsahib*, or wife, of the colonial officer. Jhal Farezi was the chicken dish made by the chefs from the leftover meat of these dinners. The Indian cooks would strip the meat from the carcass and stir-fry it in a *karai* with onion and green chiles. Any leftover roast potatoes were also cut up and added to the *karai*. Leftover roast turkey, beef, or lamb can also be cooked using this recipe. If you do not have any leftover chicken and you want to make *Jhal Farezi* from scratch, see page 64.

4 tbsp vegetable oil

1 onion, roughly cut into chunks

1-in (2.5-cm) piece of fresh root
    ginger, peeled and grated

2 whole dried red chiles

2 cups (300g) leftover roast
    chicken cut into 1-in
    (2.5-cm) strips
    *this may not be possible*
    *depending on the type of*
    *meat left over—but avoid*
    *small pieces as these will*
    *fall apart in the cooking*

½ tsp ground turmeric

½ tsp chili powder

2 fresh tomatoes, cubed

¼ green bell pepper,
    cored, seeded, and
    cut into strips

any leftover roast potatoes,
    cubed *optional*

2 fresh green chiles (medium
    spicy, with seeds left in),
    cut into rough chunks

salt, to taste

handful of cilantro leaves,
    chopped, to garnish

Heat the oil in a *karai* or wok over a medium heat. When hot, add the onion and stir-fry for 2 minutes, then add the ginger and dried red chiles and stir-fry for a further 2 minutes. Add the chicken strips followed by the turmeric and chili powder, then add the tomatoes, green pepper, and salt. Mix well in the pan to ensure everything is seasoned and spiced; taste and add more salt if required. This is a dry dish without gravy, so try not to add any water. If the mixture is sticking, add a splash of water to release them, but only use as much as you need. Add the potatoes (if using) and continue to cook until everything is well heated through. Finally, add the fresh green chiles. Serve garnished with cilantro.

# CHICKEN TONIGHT

A Midweek Dinner

Many of the meals in my home were a combination
of dishes with contrasting flavors and textures like the
*aloo makai tikki* and jhal farezi here. You can substitute
the rotis in this meal for rice, but not plain rice—you need
a moist *pulao* such as Narangi Pulao (page 207) as all
the dishes are without gravy. There is a common
misconception that most of the food in India, irrespective
of region, is "curry and rice." The word curry itself has
no cultural connotation in the subcontinent—the term
is a cultural artifact of the Raj, and was an English term
erroneously used to describe "*kari*," a south Indian gravy.
Aside from the fact that the term itself is a misnomer,
archetypal "curry and rice" does not reflect how meals are
presented across the subcontinent. Staple carbohydrates
and proteins vary wildly based on the produce available,
as well as the cultural and religious norms of a given
region. An Indian meal can be eaten from a steel *thali*,
a banana leaf, fine china, or a newspaper on the roadside.
Understanding the broad spectrum of Indian meal types
opens your horizons to exciting combinations such
as this one.

## MENU SUGGESTION

### Jhal Farezi – From Scratch
*Sweet*
PAGE 64

### Aloo Makai Tikki
*Sweet*
PAGE 65

### Hari Chatni
*(or any other chutney you may have)*
*Tangy*
PAGE 25

SERVE WITH ROTI, PITTA, STORE-BOUGHT LAVASH, OR NAAN
*(I have served with Zucchini Paratha, page 53)*

# Jhal Farezi – From Scratch

This recipe is closer to what is served in traditional British curry houses. *Jhal* is a Bengali word for spicy. The jury is out on the origin of the word *farezi*—it could be a term to describe stir-frying, or *porhezi*, meaning "fit to eat!" I guess adding chiles to roast chicken leftovers did make it fit to eat for the Bengali cooks! The bell peppers (capsicums) are fried separately and added to the chicken later, which is an unusual cooking process that helps to keep the peppers crunchy. This dish is as authentic as it is unauthentic and is a bridge that connects the two regions of the world where I am rooted: Bengal in India and London in England!

6 tbsp neutral oil

2 Indian bay leaves

2 cinnamon sticks

2 dried whole red chiles

2¼lb (1kg) boneless, skinless chicken thighs, cut into 1-in (2.5-cm) cubes

1 large white onion, cut into 1-in (2.5-cm) cubes

2 tsp salt, or to taste

1 tbsp garlic paste

2 tbsp ginger paste

½–1 tbsp red chili powder

1 tbsp Kashmiri red chili powder

1 tbsp ground coriander

1 tsp ground turmeric

1 tsp ground cumin

6 tbsp tomato paste

2 fresh tomatoes, quartered

1¾ cups (400ml) warm water

½ tsp sugar (any type)

**FOR THE PEPPERS**

2 tbsp vegetable oil

3½oz (100g) red onion, cut into 1-in (2.5-cm) cubes

1 green bell pepper, cored, seeds removed, cut into 1-in (2.5-cm) cubes

1 red bell pepper, cored, seeds removed, cut into 1-in (2.5-cm) cubes

**TO GARNISH**

handful of cilantro leaves, chopped

2 fresh green chiles, deseeded and chopped

Using a deep saucepan with a lid (you will need the lid later), warm the oil over a medium-high heat. When the oil starts to shimmer, add the bay leaves, cinnamon sticks, and dried red chiles, and stir for a few minutes, allowing their flavors to infuse into the oil. Add the chicken pieces and brown on all sides. Add the onion, salt, garlic and ginger pastes, and continue to fry for 3–4 minutes. Add the dried ground spices (adding chili powder to suit your taste—½ tbsp is the standard amount; 1 tbsp is for the brave of heart!), reduce the heat, and continue to stir, uncovered, for 10 minutes.

Add the tomato paste, fresh tomatoes, and warm water. Bring to a boil, then cover and reduce to a simmer. Cook for 10 minutes.

Meanwhile, prepare the peppers. Heat the oil in a skillet over a medium-high heat, add the red onion, followed by both peppers, and stir-fry until the peppers are still crunchy but no longer hard. Remove the onion and peppers with a slotted spoon and spread over a plate. This will prevent them continuing to cook and soften.

Remove the lid from the chicken pan and stir-fry over a high heat until the liquid has evaporated and the gravy has thickened. Add the sugar and stir well. Check that the chicken is cooked through, then add the cooked peppers and onions to the pan and mix well. Taste for seasoning and adjust, if needed.

Serve garnished with cilantro and fresh green chiles. This is a tangy dish and is best eaten with plain rice or bread, and a crunchy, salty vegetable, such as Bengali Cabbage, on page 93.

*Pictured on pages 66–67*

# Aloo Makai Tikki

POTATO AND SWEET-CORN PATTIES

I grew up in Calcutta, where no birthday party or picnic was complete without a vegetable *chop*. Potato-based chops, usually covered in breadcrumbs and deep-fried, were a popular street food in Bengal. The origins of potato and vegetable combinations mixed together to form a cylindrical croquette-shaped chop have often been traced to the Portuguese influence in India, not least because they introduced potatoes to India in the early seventeenth century. *Tikki* are a flat, disk-shaped version of potato chops and are more widely available in India. Often made on large *tawas* on carts in the street, they are served piping hot with chutney. This recipe combines two of my favorite things: potatoes and corn!

1½lb (700g) Russet potatoes

1½ cups (200g) corn kernels (raw or frozen)

1½ tbsp vegetable oil, plus extra for shallow-frying and greasing

1 tsp sesame seeds

1 tbsp fresh root ginger, peeled and finely grated

2 fresh green chiles, deseeded and finely chopped

1 tbsp roasted ground cumin (see page 29)

½ tsp Kashmiri red chili powder

½ tsp ground turmeric

1½ tsp salt

6 tbsp finely chopped cilantro leaves

4 tbsp lemon juice

*Hari Chatni* (see page 25), to serve

Boil the potatoes in their skins until tender to the point of a knife. Drain and leave to cool, then remove the skins and cut into small, even-sized cubes.

In a separate pan, boil the corn until cooked. Drain and set aside.

Heat the oil in a deep saucepan over a medium heat. Add the sesame seeds, followed by the grated ginger and chopped green chiles, and stir for a minute. Add the ground cumin, chili powder, and turmeric, and stir for 30 seconds. If the spices are catching or burning, add a spray of water and continue to stir. Add the cooked potatoes and corn, and stir-fry, then add the salt and mix, using the back of a wooden spoon to gently break up the potatoes and smooth out any lumps. Remove from the heat and stir through the chopped cilantro and lemon juice. Let cool.

With oiled hands, divide the potato mixture into 12 even-sized balls and press flat into patties. Cover and store in the fridge until you are ready to fry them—these are best eaten when freshly fried.

Heat enough oil for shallow-frying in a large skillet over a medium-high heat. Fry 2–3 *tikkis* at a time as you will need space to turn them. Fry for about 2 minutes on each side. Remove with a slotted spoon to drain on paper towels.

Serve hot, with the mint and cilantro chutney on the side.

*Pictured on pages 66–67*

# Paneer Tikka

Paneer is an underrated and versatile ingredient in so many iconic dishes in South Asia. It's one of the few ingredients that is loved by vegetarians and meat-eaters alike. The team at my restaurant fight over the leftover paneer at the end of dinner service— it's a prodigious sight! Paneer tikka kebabs are a great introduction to cooking paneer as they are relatively quick and easy.

4 tbsp mustard oil
  (or vegetable oil)
1lb 2oz (500g) paneer, cut
  into 1½-in (4-cm) cubes
1 medium onion, cut into
  1-in (2.5-cm) chunks
1 green bell pepper, cored,
  seeds removed, cut into
  1-in (2.5-cm) chunks

**FOR THE BATTER**
1¾ cups (400g) full-fat plain
  yogurt
3 tbsp lemon juice
2 tbsp chickpea flour (*besan*)
1 tbsp red chili powder/paprika *if
  you want the kebab spicier,
  you can add ¼ tsp chili/red
  pepper flakes*
1½ tsp dried fenugreek
  (*kasuri methi*)
1½ tsp salt
1 tsp ginger paste
1 tsp garlic paste
1 tsp freshly ground
  black pepper
1 tsp ground turmeric
1 tsp ground coriander
1 tsp roasted cumin seed
  powder (see page 29
  or use store-bought)
1 tsp crushed carom
  seeds (*ajwain*)

**EQUIPMENT**
4–5 thick metal skewers

Combine all the ingredients for the batter in a large bowl and whisk until smooth.

Heat 2 tbsp of the mustard oil in a small pan over a high heat. When very hot, carefully pour the oil into the batter (this step is optional, but it really helps release the complexity of the spices in the batter). Alternatively, add the mustard oil cold if you do not want to go through the hassle of heating it. Give the batter a minute to cool, then add the paneer cubes, mixing gently until all the pieces are equally covered. Add the onion and pepper chunks, and stir again to ensure an even coating. Cover the bowl with plastic wrap and refrigerate for at least 2 hours.

Take a thick metal skewer and start by skewering a piece of onion, then pepper, and lastly a piece of paneer. Repeat this process until the skewer is made up to your desired size and all your ingredients are used up. Here are two methods I recommend for cooking:

TO OVEN BAKE   Preheat the oven to 425°F (220°C). Place the skewers on a wire rack set over a baking sheet and bake for 15–20 minutes, or until browned all over.

OPTIONAL STEP   Remove from the oven and, holding the end of each skewer with an oven glove or dish towel, char the kebabs directly over the flame of a gas stove to give them a beautiful smoky flavor.

TO BARBECUE   Heat your barbecue grill to a medium heat and cook the kebabs, turning until evenly golden brown. This will add that desirable smokiness by default, and is a great way to impress a mixed crowd of vegetarians and meat-eaters without having to prep two separate dishes on two different parts of your barbecue.

# Shrikhand

### YOGURT WITH SAFFRON AND PISTACHIO

*Shrikhand* is a great gluten-free dessert of Gujarati origin that can be made in advance and requires little fuss to prepare. It's a great one to involve younger children with, as there is almost no cooking over heat and enough messy action to make little ones happy (and all the ingredients are safe to eat from the very start). You can adapt it by adding seasonal fruits on top instead of the traditional nuts. I love eating this with chopped mangoes and my kids have it with blackberries and raspberries.

3 cups (750g) full-fat
    plain yogurt
1 tsp full-fat milk
large pinch of good-quality
    saffron threads
1 cup (200g) granulated sugar
1½ tsp ground cardamom
    *if making it yourself, you will*
    *need to use the seeds from*
    *quite a few cardamom pods*
    *to get a powder—store the*
    *extra in an airtight container*
    *to use for another recipe*
3 tbsp slivered almonds
    and pistachios
    (store-bought is okay)

**EQUIPMENT**
cheesecloth for straining

Start at least 6–8 hours before you want to serve. Rinse the cheesecloth and squeeze it well to get rid of any excess water, then drape it over a bowl with the edges hanging out. Transfer the yogurt to the middle of the cheesecloth and bring the edges of the cloth together. Twist until the yogurt collects at the bottom and you can tie a knot at the top. Hang the cheesecloth over the sink or any other container—the yogurt must be hanging to be able to drain the excess whey properly. If the kitchen is too hot to leave the yogurt safely, find a cool part of the house in which to drain it.

Close to the end of the draining time, prepare the saffron-infused milk. Warm the milk to tepid (the saffron will lose its floral aroma if the milk is too hot), then soak the saffron threads in the milk. Set aside.

Once the yogurt is drained, transfer it to a bowl and beat well with a whisk. Sprinkle with the sugar and ground cardamom, and continue to mix. Finally, add the saffron-infused milk and stir. Taste to check whether it is sweet is enough—*shrikhand* is tangy, but sweetness is essential. Transfer the *shrikhand* to a serving bowl, cover with plastic wrap, and chill in the fridge before serving.

Serve decorated with the slivered nuts.

# Zaffran Lassi

SAFFRON-INFUSED LASSI

A churned sweet yogurt and water drink, *lassi* can range from sweet to salty to something in between. The origin of this drink has commonly been attributed to the North Indian state of Punjab, a land abundant with milk due to the large number of dairy farmers, helped by the lush vegetation and climate. *Lassi* is a popular drink in the fiery hot summer months, as it cools down the body. In winter, it is drunk along with rich and spicy warming food. The *lactobacillus* bacteria in the *lassi* (from the yogurt) helps to break down food and counter acidity in the gut. A small amount of infused saffron here gives this *lassi* a beautiful and delicate flavor.

⅛ tsp good-quality saffron
   threads
1 tbsp warm milk
4 cups (1kg) full-fat thick
   plain yogurt
⅓ cup (80g) granulated
   sugar, or to taste
1 cup (225ml) water,
   or as needed
crushed ice, to serve

In a bowl, infuse the saffron threads in the warm milk. Set aside for at least 30 minutes.

Whisk the yogurt with the sugar until the sugar has dissolved, then whisk in the saffron-infused milk. Add some or all of the water, if necessary—the *lassi* should be the consistency of heavy cream (remember it will thicken slightly in the fridge). Taste and add more sugar to suit your preference.

Chill until ready to serve over crushed ice.

# SUMMER GARDEN PARTY

Vegetarian

All these dishes can be prepared in advance and are
easy to serve; they also scale up well, so you can just
multiply the quantities if you have a larger group.
Summer is mango season in the subcontinent and using
ripe mangoes to make the *kulfi* and raw mangoes to make
the pungent *aam panna* drink is a great way to showcase
the range of flavors and versatility of seasonal mango
cultivars. The softness of the *dahi vada* (lentil fritters)
with the spiced creamy yogurt dressing is a good partner
to the tangy and textured *chotpoti* (white peas). The
combination of these two dishes is reminiscent of street
foods like *dahi papri chaat* and *dahi puchkas*—a mix
of sweet and tangy with delightful pockets
of crunchiness.

## MENU SUGGESTION

**Chotpoti**
*Pungent*
PAGE 76

**Dahi Vada**
*Sour*
PAGE 78

**Mango Kulfi**
*Sweet*
PAGE 79

**Aam Panna**
*Sour*
PAGE 82

# Chotpoti

SPICY, TANGY WHITE PEAS

Over a couple of generations, we seem to have limited the range of ingredients we use for our cooking. The overcultivation of certain foods, like corn, wheat, and rice, will have a long-term impact on our environment. This dish is a great way to expand our repertoire. Legumes are rich in nutrients, and in Ayurveda are considered to be astringent in flavor. White peas were harvested for centuries in northern and western India, and are high in zinc and phosphorus. They can also be used as a substitute for white chickpeas in other dishes. If you like, you could also add a sprinkle of chopped green chiles to this dish, for a little heat.

½lb (225g) dried white peas
½ tsp baking powder
3½oz (100g) Yukon Gold potato
1 small cucumber
1 tomato
1 tsp salt
3 tbsp chopped onion
1 boiled egg, sliced
2 tbsp chopped cilantro leaves

FOR THE TAMARIND CHUTNEY
2 tsp cumin seeds
2 dried red chiles
1½ cups (350ml) water
2 golf-ball–sized pieces of
    dried tamarind pulp
3 tbsp sugar (any type)
½ tsp kala namak
    (Himalayan rock salt)
¼ tsp salt, or to taste

Soak the dried peas in water with the baking powder for at least 4 hours or ideally overnight.

Drain the soaked peas, rinse under cold running water, and drain again. Place in a pan with plenty of fresh water and bring to a boil, then cover and simmer until the peas are tender, up to 1 hour.

Meanwhile, boil the potato in its skin until tender, then drain and cool. Remove the skin and cut into small cubes. Chop the cucumber and tomato to match the size of the potato cubes. Set aside.

Dry-roast the cumin seeds and dried chiles (for the tamarind chutney) in a heavy-based skillet until they darken a couple of shades. Transfer to a plate to cool and then grind to a powder in a spice grinder. Set aside.

When the peas are cooked, drain and transfer to a bowl. Add the salt and mix.

For the tamarind chutney, boil the measured water, add the dried tamarind pulp, and bring to a gentle boil. Reduce the heat to a simmer and cook the tamarind uncovered over a low heat for 15 minutes. Remove from the heat and leave to cool.

When cool enough to touch, use your hands to pulp the rehydrated tamarind and ensure all the tamarind pulp is released from the seeds and pod. Strain the tamarind pulp into a bowl and add the roasted cumin and chili powder, sugar, kala namak, and salt. Mix well. Taste and adjust the balance of sweet, salty, and tangy. (If you can't get dried tamarind pulp, you can use tamarind concentrate, but this will be at the expense of flavor.)

Mix the potatoes, cucumber, tomatoes, and chopped onion into the peas. Add the tamarind chutney and mix well. Garnish with sliced egg and chopped cilantro, and serve.

# Dahi Vada

LENTIL FRITTERS IN A SPICED YOGURT

This combination of *vada*, deep-fried fritters made with a dough of split black lentils, and spiced yogurt, is popular in North and South India, both as a home-cooked dish and as street food. At some point, these two food items were combined to make this dish. Yogurt is often eaten as part of a meal to help counter the heat of chiles or to help with digestion and gut health.

½ cup (100g) split skinless black gram (*urad dal*)

½ cup (100g) split skinless moong dal

3 cups (750ml) water, to soak, plus ½ cup (120ml) for the paste

1-in (2.5-cm) fresh root ginger, peeled and roughly chopped

2 green chiles, deseeded and roughly chopped

1 tsp salt

pinch of baking soda

15–20 raisins, finely chopped

2 tbsp blanched cashew nuts, finely chopped

vegetable oil, for deep-frying

TO SERVE

2 cups (500g) full-fat plain yogurt, chilled

2 tsp roasted ground cumin (see page 29)

¼ tsp salt

½ tsp Himalayan rock salt

1 tbsp sugar (any type)

*Hari Chatni* (see page 25)

Tamarind Chutney (see page 76)

¼ tsp chili powder

2 tbsp chopped cilantro leaves

Place the dals in separate bowls filled with cold water and rub the lentils between your fingers to thoroughly clean. Discard the cloudy water, replenish with fresh cold water, and continue to wash the lentils. You may need to change the water a few times until it is no longer cloudy. At this point, leave each dal to soak in the 3 cups of water—overnight in warmer climates, or 48 hours in cooler climates.

In a food processor, blitz together the fresh ginger, green chiles, and salt until you have a paste. Drain and rinse the soaked dals, then drain again and add them to the food processor. Blitz to combine. Continue to blitz while slowly adding the ½ cup of water, scraping down the sides of the processor with a silicone spatula from time to time, until you have a light and fluffy batter. Transfer the batter to a bowl, cover with plastic wrap, and set aside in a warm place for 30 minutes.

Add a pinch of baking soda to the batter along with the raisins and cashews, and gently fold in. Divide the batter into 18 equal portions (each about 2½–3 tbsp) and place on a piece of parchment paper. Fill a deep bowl with warm water and set next to the stove.

Heat a 3in (8cm) depth of oil in a deep saucepan or *karai* over a medium heat. When the oil is shimmering, flatten 4 portions of the batter into biscuit-sized patties. Use a wooden spatula to gently float them into the hot oil. Fry for about 2 minutes until brown on one side, then flip over and brown the other sides. Carefully remove and completely immerse in the warm water. Leave to soak for 10 minutes, then remove and squeeze out any excess liquid between your hands. Set aside, covered. Repeat until all the *vadas* are fried and soaked.

When ready to serve, plate 3 *vadas* per person. Whisk the yogurt in a bowl along with the roasted ground cumin, salt, rock salt, and sugar until smooth. Pour half of the yogurt mixture over the *vadas*, then gently turn them over and pour over the remaining yogurt. Drizzle the coriander and tamarind chutneys on top, sprinkle with chili powder, and finish with the chopped cilantro.

The *vadas* can also be made in advance, then covered and refrigerated for 24 hours. Serve chilled or bring to room temperature before serving.

*Pictured on page 77*

# Mango Kulfi

This recipe is an adaptation of my mother's mango ice cream, which was made using an old wooden barrel churn, with a handle on the side that had to be cranked by hand. When we were young, my siblings and I would take turns churning the ice cream to guarantee additional scoops of it when it was ready! The mangoes I grew up eating were mainly the phenomenal Langra mangoes that grew around Calcutta, the skin of which remains green even when ripe. Langra was also the variety of mangoes grown in my father's orchard in Uttar Pradesh. The combination of lime with the sweetness of the mango works well in this dish. If you are unable to get mangoes where you live, they can be replaced by any soft fruit that can be pulped, such as raspberries. This recipe allows you to make authentic homemade *kulfi* without an ice-cream machine.

3½ cups (850g) canned
   evaporated milk
1 cup (200g) granulated sugar
1¾lb (800g) mangoes, peeled
   and freshly pulped (see Note)
juice of ½ lime

In a heavy-based saucepan, heat the milk slowly over a medium heat. Bring to a boil, then reduce to a low, controlled simmer. Add the sugar a tablespoon at a time, and stir gently to help it dissolve. Once the sugar has dissolved, remove from the heat and leave to cool.

When the milk has cooled, mix with the mango pulp and lime juice. Pour the mixture into a traditional cone-shaped *kulfi* mold, a popsicle mold, or ice-cube trays. Freeze for 1 hour until set.

Remove the *kulfi* from the freezer and break it up with a fork to smooth out any ice chips, then return it to the freezer for 4 hours.

Before serving, remove the *kulfi* from the freezer a few minutes beforehand, so it softens a little.

NOTE   Peel the mangoes and use your hands to squeeze the flesh, which will—depending on the ripeness of the mangoes—come out in chunks or a paste. Squeeze the stone of the mangoes to get all the fruit and juice out. Use your hands to break up the lumps, then blend or whisk to a smooth pulp.

*Pictured on page 81*

# Aam Panna

### A RAW-MANGO DRINK

The weeks before the monsoon rains in India are a sweltering fight with dehydration. Stillness and humidity make these long days exhausting: you sweat out any water you drink, and the lack of breeze means you just don't cool down. *Aam panna* is a refreshing and hydrating raw-mango drink, which was traditionally used to help fight fatigue in the high summer. Raw mangoes are packed with vitamin C, which boosts immunity. The addition of salt in this drink helps to replenish body salts lost due to humidity. Once the raw mango is roasted and the pulp taken out, the base of the *aam panna* can be stored in the fridge and used for a couple of days to make the drink when desired.

A big determinant of the overall flavor profile and appearance of *aam panna* is how you choose to sweeten it. White sugar, unrefined cane sugar, and evaporated sugar cane juice are all traditional choices and will all result in a well-balanced drink. My personal favorite method to sweetening my syrup is to make a syrup out of jaggery (*gur).* This makes, for me, the quintessential, authentic *aam panna*.

2¼ lb (1kg) fresh raw (green) mangoes (about 1 cup of pulp)
1 tsp cumin seeds, roasted (see page 29)
¼ tsp black salt
1 cup (200g) jaggery (or white granulated sugar, unrefined cane sugar, or evaporated sugar cane juice), as needed (see method)

**TO SERVE**
crushed ice
water, as needed
whole green chiles, to garnish

Start by charring your mangoes. There are a few options on how to do this, based on the equipment you have available. If you have a *tawa* or large, cast-iron skillet, heat your raw mangoes over a medium heat, covered by a lid. Turn the mangoes periodically to ensure they are blackened on all sides. You can also char your mangoes directly over an open flame on a gas stove or even a barbecue grill. You can hold the mangoes with a skewer or place them on a metal grate. Lastly, if you have access to neither a *tawa* nor an open flame, you can use the broiler in your oven set to a high heat to get the same char on your mangoes. They are done when a knife can pierce them with little to no resistance. Mangoes vary wildly between varieties in size and juice content, so your cook time will vary depending on what classification of mango you use. Rajapuri mangoes are a good choice for their *khatta meetha* (sweet and sour) flavor.

Once your mangoes are evenly blackened, score their skins and set aside to cool until you can comfortably handle them.

Meanwhile, roast the cumin seeds (see page 29 for detailed instructions). I like roasted cumin in my *aam panna*—it adds a complex earthiness to the drink that complements its sweet and sour flavors.

The scored skins should be very easy to remove from your scorched mangoes. Remove as much pulp from the mango as you can, using a spoon to scrape the skins and a small knife to remove as much pulp as you can from the stone. I like to be vigorous when scraping the skins as these are rich in tannins that can add astringency to your drink. If you don't want this, be careful not to scrape the skin too hard. Add this pulp, the roasted cumin, and black salt to a blender and blitz to a smooth pulp (you may need to add some water to achieve a smooth paste). Measure the resulting amount of pulp.

Add the same volume of jaggery (or other sweetener) as you have mango pulp (i.e., for every tablespoon of pulp add a tablespoon of jaggery) to a saucepan and melt over a medium-high heat. Once it has completely melted, carefully pour the contents of the pan into your concentrate and blend to combine once more.

Strain the concentrate and store in a clean, airtight jar. This will last for around 1 week in the fridge or 1 month in the freezer (see Note below).

To serve, add some crushed ice to a glass, add 2 tablespoons of concentrate and 1 cup (225ml) water, and stir until combined. You can also make this in a large jug or pitcher where it can be stored, covered, in the fridge for a couple of days. Use a ratio of 1 tablespoon of concentrate per ½ cup (100ml) water. Garnish with a whole green chile.

NOTE    This recipe makes a simple, sweet and sour *aam panna*. You can add more depth to your drink by blending in fresh ginger juice or mint leaves, but keep in mind if you add fresh ingredients to your concentrate you will only be able to store it in the fridge for 2 days. You can also try using nontraditional sweeteners, such as agave or coconut sugar, to achieve a different flavor profile. Sweetening is not mandatory—*khatta*, or sour, *aam panna* is served without any sweetener, but this is an acquired taste.

*Pictured on pages 80–81*

বর্ষা

2

# BÔRSHA

## Monsoon

Monsoon—my favorite season—brings with it a symphony of rhythmic, relentless rain. There's something deeply comforting about sitting by the window, listening to the rain's soothing melody, while sharing steaming hot pakoras and *chai* with my siblings. Those cozy afternoons are among my fondest memories. The monsoon rain nourishes the earth, washing away the dust of summer, and in doing so it seems to cleanse my spirit, too. The air becomes cool, the greenery refreshed, and everything feels new again.

Monsoon dishes, much like the season itself, are warming and healing. From richly spiced curries and stews to crispy fritters, they offer comfort on rainy days. These dishes are often served with hot, spiced *chai*, elevating the experience into a celebration of the senses. As we eat, laugh, and share stories, monsoon feels like more than just a season—it becomes a reminder of the simple joys of life.

# Monsoon Pakoras

This is a basic batter for pakoras. You can add any of the following to the batter: thinly sliced potatoes, thinly sliced cauliflower, chopped spinach or spinach leaves, sliced onions, whole mild chiles, sliced eggplant, sliced hard-boiled eggs, shredded cabbage, or chopped zucchini, and deep-fry them to make a monsoon pakora. An accompanying chutney is important—the Hari Chatni (page 25) or Tamarind Chutney (page 76) are both great with pakoras. You can also use a store-bought sweet and sour or chili sauce as an accompaniment.

¾ cup (200g) gram flour (*besan*)

1 tsp salt

1 tsp ground cumin

½ tsp ground turmeric

½ tsp chili powder

pinch of chili flakes

1 tsp arrowroot or cornstarch

¼ tsp baking soda

½ tsp carom (*ajwain*) seeds, crushed *optional*

⅔ cup (150ml) water

1 cup (250ml) vegetable oil, or any neutral cooking oil

10oz (300g) chosen pakora ingredient (see list in recipe introduction, above)

To make the batter, add the gram flour, salt, cumin, turmeric, chili powder, chili flakes, arrowroot or cornstarch, baking soda, and *ajwain* (if using) to a large bowl and slowly mix in the water to make a smooth, thick, lump-free batter.

NOTE    If you are using sliced eggplant, salt the slices for 10 minutes and squeeze out the excess liquid before adding to the batter. You can be adventurous and finely chop or grate any vegetable to make a pakora. It's important that it is cut in such a way that it will cook in the brief time it is fried.

While preparing the batter, heat the oil in a large, heavy-based pan over a medium-low heat. Once you are ready to fry, increase the heat under the pan to high. Dip your chosen pakora ingredient into the batter and coat well, then carefully lower the pakora into the oil. Turn with a slotted spoon to ensure it is evenly cooked and crisp on both sides, then remove to a wire rack while you fry the rest. This will keep them crisp and prevent them from becoming soggy.

A TIP ON FRYING PAKORAS    Do not drop the pakora from a height—the splash as the pakora hits the oil may burn your hand. Take the coated pakora to the edge of the pan, just above the oil level and gently drop it in. I always fry one pakora at a time. This ensures the oil stays at a stable temperature, comes back to temperature quickly between frying each one, and the pakoras do not clump together, saving you time in the long run.

# SOOTHING SUPPER

## The Introspection Meal

This is the perfect meal for when you decide to stay home, and have time to cook and think. A day when you plan to do nothing. I know this kind of a day is a luxury for many of us, but it is vital for our emotional well-being. Too many of us—especially women who have families to look after or elderly parents, or who work in toxic environments and are constantly battling to stay in one place, or those carrying burdens of grief and pain—often burn themselves out to keep others warm. Yes, you can be the healer and the feeder, but you cannot always run on empty. This is the meal you need to invest in for your well-being. The flavors of the cabbage and the railway curry are a great contrast. Ideally, eat them with plain rice, as you do not want to bring more flavors to the meal. Absorb the healing spices, use your favorite plate to eat from, watch that sitcom that used to make you laugh when you were younger—and enjoy your dinner!

MENU SUGGESTION

**First-Class Railway Curry**
*Sweet*
PAGE 92

**Bengali Cabbage**
*Pungent*
PAGE 93

SERVE WITH RICE

# First-Class Railway Curry

The origin of this mild beef curry with coconut milk, as its name implies, was the Indian Railways dining car. During colonial times, this dish was created for the English passengers traveling in first class as a change from the standard English meal of meat (usually mutton chops) and two veg, which was prepared specially for them. The popular story is that an English passenger was tempted to try the standard mutton curry the staff were eating and enjoyed the flavors but not the chiles. The cooks added coconut milk to the gravy to temper it down. The addition of vinegar to this dish was possibly to preserve the meat for longer. The potatoes are meant to be cut in large chunks, which is popular in Bengal. You can use stewing beef, mutton leg pieces, or lamb shanks to make this dish.

4 tbsp vegetable oil

1½-in (4-cm) cassia bark
    (or cinnamon stick)

3 cloves

3 green cardamom pods

1 Indian bay (cassia) leaf

1 dried red chile

2¼ lb (1kg) beef stew meat/
    mutton/lamb shanks

2 small onions, finely chopped,
    then crushed to a paste

4 garlic cloves, crushed to a
    paste

1 tbsp fresh ginger paste

½ tsp ground turmeric

1½ tsp ground coriander

1½ tsp ground cumin

1 tomato, diced

2 tsp salt

4 tbsp malt vinegar,
    or more to taste

3 cups (700ml) water

2 large Russet potatoes,
    peeled and quartered

1 x 13.5 oz (400ml) can
    coconut milk

1 whole green chile *optional*,
    to garnish

In a heavy-based pan that has a lid, heat the oil over a medium to high heat. Add the cassia bark, cloves, cardamom pods, bay leaf, and dried red chile. Stir until the spices and the chile have darkened in color, then use a slotted spoon to remove the spices to a plate and set aside.

In the same chile-infused oil, brown the meat pieces on all sides. Do not allow the meat to cook through; the aim is just to brown the meat. Remove the meat from the pan and set aside, leaving as much of the oil in the pan as possible.

Add the onions, and garlic and ginger pastes to the pan. Take care as the pastes will splutter in the hot oil. Next, add the ground spices followed by the diced tomato and cook for 2 minutes, before returning the whole fried spices and browned meat to the pan. Add the salt, vinegar, and measured water, and bring to the boil. After 1 minute, cover the pan with the lid and reduce to a simmer. After about 1 hour, when the meat is three-quarters cooked (it should be soft, but not falling apart, and the edges should be curled), add the potatoes and stir to coat with the gravy. Stir at regular intervals to ensure the potatoes are cooking evenly—do not shake them too much as they may break.

Once the meat and potatoes are cooked, remove the lid, and reduce any remaining liquid until the oil seeps to the edges of the pan. Usually, I add some vinegar at this stage too—it depends on whether the vinegar aroma was lost in the cooking process. Add the coconut milk and taste for seasoning before serving.

*Pictured on page 90*

# Bengali Cabbage

This is a recipe for Bengali-style cabbage, but it will work for just about any vegetable: green beans, snap peas, and even steamed curly or Tuscan kale can all be used as substitutes for the cabbage. The quick and simple method makes it an ideal side dish or midweek meal. I like to have this cabbage as a side to a rich, gravy-based curry. It's a great way to bulk out your meal and increase your vegetable intake.

½ white cabbage
    (about 1lb 2oz/500g)
3 tbsp vegetable oil or ghee
1 tsp black mustard seeds
4 garlic cloves, finely chopped
2 dried red chiles, broken in half
1 tsp ground turmeric
1½ tsp salt
1 tbsp lemon juice, or to taste

Cut your cabbage in half lengthways and remove the core, then cut each half across from top to bottom making thin slices.

Heat the oil in a deep pan or wok over a medium-high heat. Add the mustard seeds and wait for these to pop, then add the garlic, dried chiles, and lastly, the sliced cabbage, stirring well. Add the turmeric and salt, and stir-fry until the cabbage is cooked.

Add lemon juice to taste, then plate and serve.

*Pictured on page 90*

# Anglo-Indian Aloo Chop

POTATOES STUFFED WITH MINCED MEAT

You may be surprised at the lack of spices and chiles in this dish. This is a traditional Anglo-Indian potato chop, which many of us grew up eating in Calcutta. The only seasoning used was salt and pepper. I have had versions of this dish where some chili powder was added to the stuffing–so you could add ½ teaspoon of chili powder while cooking the meat. In our house, *aloo chop* was always served with buttered toast. I would dip it into tomato ketchup, while my sister would add chili sauce as a condiment. Leftovers were mashed and used as a sandwich filling, and put into our tiffin box the next day. The oval shape of this chop seems to be an important part of its culinary heritage. Most other chops we ate in Bengal were either cylindrical croquettes or flat like a patty. Once you are confident with the recipe, feel free to experiment and add more things.

2¼lb (1kg) potatoes (such as Russets)
2 tbsp salted butter
½ tsp salt
½ tsp freshly ground black pepper
2 tbsp plain flour *optional, if required*
1 egg, beaten
1 cup (80g) fine breadcrumbs
vegetable oil, for shallow-frying

**FOR THE STUFFING**
2 tbsp vegetable oil
1 large bay leaf
1 medium onion, finely chopped
½ tsp ginger paste
½ tsp garlic paste
½lb (225g) ground meat
*we used mutton, but lean lamb or beef can be used too*
1 tsp salt
½ tsp freshly ground black pepper

Set the potatoes to boil in their skins in a large pan of water.

Meanwhile, prepare the stuffing. Heat the oil in a frying pan over a medium-high heat. Add the bay leaf, then the onion, and stir-fry until they darken to a golden brown. Add the ginger and garlic pastes and continue to stir until the raw smell goes away, about 2 minutes. If the contents are getting stuck in the pan, spray with a little water. Add the meat and use the back of a wooden spoon to break up any lumps. Season with the salt and pepper. Once the meat has browned, add enough water to cover and bring to a boil, then cover and reduce to a simmer. Cook for 10–15 minutes. Check the meat has cooked through, then cook uncovered over a medium-high heat to evaporate any remaining moisture. The stuffing needs to be dry in texture. Remove and discard the bay leaf, then check the seasoning and let cool.

Keep checking on the potatoes periodically. Once they are fork tender, drain and let cool. Remove the skins and mash with a fork or a potato ricer, then add the butter, salt, and pepper, and mix well. Transfer to a bowl, cover with plastic wrap, and set aside (do not refrigerate).

Divide the mashed potatoes into 12 portions. You may need to add the flour and mix if the mash is too sticky. Dampening both hands makes it easier to shape the chops. Flatten each portion of potato into a disk and place 1 teaspoon of the stuffing mixture into the middle. Close the chop around the filling and form into a flat oval shape (one end needs to be more pointy while the other end is rounded).

Place the beaten egg in a shallow bowl and the breadcrumbs on a plate. Dip each chop in the beaten egg with one hand, and then transfer to the breadcrumbs and use the other hand to cover with the crumb. Repeat this process until all the chops are coated with crumb. Place in a covered container and refrigerate for 1 hour.

Heat enough oil for shallow-frying in a skillet over a medium heat (fill the skillet about halfway). Fry the chops, 3–4 at a time, until brown and crispy on both sides. Eat immediately.

# Quick Bengali Murgir Korma

CHICKEN IN A MILD YOGURT GRAVY

This is a mild chicken *korma* we would make at home when there was leftover yogurt in the house. Usually, *kormas* were made for special occasions and feasts, and had additions of nuts, saffron, and raisins. This recipe is a comforting everyday recipe that can be made quickly and requires few ingredients to prepare. I have added a bit of chili powder, which is often omitted in many Bengali households. *Korma* is a mild dish and adding excessive chiles will take away from the mild and sweet flavor of the dish.

1¾lb (800g) bone-in or
   1½lb (650g) boneless
   chicken thighs
2 tbsp ginger paste
1 tbsp garlic paste
½ cup (100g) full-fat
   plain yogurt
½ cup (100g) vegetable oil
½ cup (150g) Spanish onion,
   thinly sliced into half-moons
1 tbsp ghee *optional*
4 green cardamom pods
4 cloves
2-in (5-cm) cassia bark
   (or cinnamon stick)
2 bay leaves
½ tsp chili powder
1 tsp salt
1¼ cup (300ml)
   warm water
1 tsp sugar (any type)

If you are using boneless chicken thighs, cut them into even-sized pieces, 2-in (5-cm) square. If you cut the pieces too small, they will break and disintegrate if you don't reduce the cooking time. The most important thing is to ensure that all the chicken pieces are the same size. This also applies to on-the-bone chicken thighs. If the thighs are of different sizes, cut the bigger thigh in half so it cooks at the same rate as the rest. If the pieces are uneven, bigger pieces need longer to cook and smaller pieces start to fall apart while the bigger pieces are still cooking.

Mix the ginger and garlic pastes into the yogurt, add the chicken pieces, and coat well, then cover and set aside for 30 minutes. (If you refrigerate the chicken, remember to bring to room temperature before cooking.)

Heat the oil in a deep saucepan with a lid over a medium heat until shimmering. Add the sliced onions and stir-fry until they are dark brown and the edges are looking crispy. Be patient and keep stirring to ensure the onions are cooked evenly. Remove with a slotted spoon to a plate and spread them out to cool and crisp up. Try to leave as much of the oil behind in the pan as possible.

Put the pan back over a medium-high heat and add the ghee (if using). When hot, add the whole spices and stir for a few seconds. Add the chicken to the pan, stir well, then add the chili powder and salt. Crush half of the browned onions and add to the pan along with the warm water. Stir and bring to the boil, then cover and reduce to a simmer. Cook until the edges of the chicken thigh curl. If using on-the-bone chicken, check after 20 minutes. Boneless chicken cooks faster, so pierce a piece to test– if the juices run clear, the chicken is ready. Add the sugar and stir to dissolve it, then taste for seasoning.

Garnish the *korma* with the remaining browned onions and serve.

# RAINY DAY
# LUNCH

Nostalgia

During monsoon season in Calcutta, after days
of relentless downpour, there would be the inevitable
flooding, with knee-high water in the gullies and by-lanes
of the city. The bazaars would be closed and often the only
delivery we could get was eggs from the *anda-wallah,* the
egg man who would pull his cycle through the water and
sell eggs direct to your home, at a substantial monsoon
premium! You do not need to wait to be flooded—the
combination of these two dishes is a real pick-me-up meal.
You can add some thick slices of cucumber or tomato
on the side, if you have any at home. The omelette curry
can be eaten the next day with rice, if you have any
leftovers. I have no suggestion for leftover paratha, as
there is never any leftover in my house! I use any straggly
bits of paratha that may be left to layer with jam,
honey, or chocolate spread, and that is my dessert.

MENU SUGGESTION

**Omelette Curry**
*Pungent*
PAGE 100

**Paratha**
*Sweet*
PAGE 101

# Omelette Curry

In Bengal, eggs are not just a breakfast item—they are served as a main course in a family meal. In my family, we ate eggs in every season, especially in monsoon when the bazaar was closed due to floods and the eggs would be delivered to our house. We usually ate this omelette-based curry with toast or bread rolls with lavish amounts of Amul butter. (Amul butter is still my all-time favorite butter. Introduced by the Kaira District Co-operative Milk Producers Union in 1946, this iconic dairy cooperative is still a household favorite in India.) As a variation, poached or fried eggs can be added to the gravy instead.

**FOR THE GRAVY**

½ cup (100ml) vegetable oil

1-in (2.5-cm) cassia bark
(or cinnamon stick)

2 bay leaves

½ cup (150g) Spanish onion,
thinly sliced

1 tbsp ginger paste

1 tsp garlic paste

½ lb (225g) fresh tomatoes,
chopped

1 tsp chili powder

1 tsp salt

½ tsp sugar (any type)

½ cup (120ml) water

1 tbsp lemon juice

**FOR THE OMELETTE**

6 large eggs

2 tbsp vegetable oil

¼ tsp salt

¼ tsp freshly ground
black pepper

3 green chiles, deseeded
and finely chopped

2 tbsp chopped fresh
cilantro leaves

Start by preparing the gravy. Heat the oil in a deep saucepan over a medium-low heat. Add the cassia bark and bay leaves, followed by the sliced onions. Stir the onions until they start to turn dark brown, ensuring they cook evenly. Add the ginger and garlic pastes, and stir for a minute. Add the chopped tomatoes and stir for a few minutes before adding the chili powder, salt, and sugar. Add the measured water and bring to a boil, then cover and reduce to a simmer.

While the gravy is simmering, prepare the omelette. It maybe easier to make two omelettes if you have a small or medium frying pan. Whisk the eggs in a bowl. Heat the oil in a frying pan over a medium heat. Add the salt and pepper to the eggs and whisk again before pouring into the pan. Sprinkle over the green chiles and cilantro, and cook until the eggs are set. Remove from the pan and set aside to cool.

When cool to the touch, cut the omelette into thick strips. Ideally you want to have six thick strips. If you cut the strips too thin, they will break up and disintegrate in the gravy.

Remove the lid from the gravy and stir. If there is still a lot of liquid, increase the heat and let it evaporate. The gravy should have the consistency of thick soup. Add the omelette strips and stir to cover all the strips with the gravy. Add the lemon juice, taste for seasoning, and serve warm.

*Pictured on page 98*

# Paratha

This is not an everyday bread eaten in homes in India, but it is often served on the weekend or for meals with visitors. The process to make parathas is ideally suited to indulgent meals where the resting period between each stage of the paratha can be used to prepare the rest of the food. Unusually, paratha is a popular bread for breakfast. The dough is enriched with oil/ghee and is twisted and rolled to form layers. The smell of parathas cooking is one of my most nostalgic food memories—the final stages as the paratha gets brown flecks and the ghee is sizzling around the edges is an aroma that immediately takes me back to my family kitchen in Calcutta.

4 cups (500g) plain flour
½ tsp salt
½ tsp baking soda
1 egg
1 tsp sugar (any type)
¾ cup (200ml) vegetable oil
1 cup (240ml) water
1 tbsp neutral oil for cooking

Sift the flour into a bowl, add the salt and baking soda, and mix.

In a separate bowl, whisk together the egg, sugar, and 3 tablespoons of the oil. Add to the flour and mix well until fully incorporated. The flour will look like crumbs at this stage. Slowly start to add the measured water and gather the flour together to make a soft and pliable dough. Cover the dough with a film of oil, cover with a damp cloth, and set aside for 2 hours.

Knock the dough back, then knead and divide the mixture into 12 small balls. Roll to ensure the balls are tight and seamless. Rub the balls with more oil, cover, and set aside for another hour.

On an oiled work surface, stretch each ball into an oval shape by hand, and then scrunch into a fanlike shape by pinching the dough together to form an accordion-style zigzag. Curl the folded strip of dough into a tight swirl and tuck in the end. Cover the swirled parathas as you work on the others.

Heat a *tawa* or flat skillet over a medium heat.

Roll each paratha into a round disk, around ¼-in (5-mm) thick. Place on the hot pan, one at a time, and cook on each side until flecked with brown. Add a small drizzle of oil around the edges of the paratha when flipping it, if needed. Serve hot.

If you are making these in advance, do not allow the parathas to cook all the way through. Cook on each side until light brown. Store with pieces of parchment paper layered between them. When ready to eat, heat over a medium-low heat until the paratha is flecked with brown.

*Pictured on page 98*

# Chawal Ki Roti

### RICE-FLOUR ROTI

This soft rice-flour roti is a wonderful alternative for anyone looking for a new kind of bread to eat with Indian food. It is very versatile—it can be eaten for breakfast, spread with a simple chutney as a snack, or served as an accompaniment to a rich meat gravy. Making the roti requires a bit of practice, but even if the shape is not perfect, it will still taste good! Rice flour can be a hit-and-miss experience, so buy small bags and try different brands before you find one that you like. Unlike other flours, this flour has to be "cooked" with hot water to enable it to produce a pliable dough.

2½ cups (600ml) water
1 tsp coconut oil
½ tsp salt
½ tsp white sugar
2 cups (350g) fine rice
flour *try to find one*
*that is roasted*
plain flour, for dusting

Bring the measured water to a rolling boil in a saucepan, then add the coconut oil, salt, and sugar, and stir with a strong wooden spoon until they dissolve. Add the rice flour and start to stir in one direction. Once it starts to come together, remove from the heat and continue to stir until it has gathered into a mass. There may be lumps in the flour, so use the back of the spoon to break them up. When the water has been fully absorbed by the rice flour, cover the pan with a kitchen towel and let rest for 5 minutes.

Transfer the dough to a flour-dusted work surface and knead for 3–4 minutes. Divide the dough into 12 balls. Placing each ball of dough between two sheets of parchment paper, use a rolling pin to roll into a circular roti, each about ⅛-in (2-mm) thick. Don't worry about achieving a perfect round.

Heat a *tawa* or large frying pan over a medium heat. Cook each roti for 1 minute on each side, then fold into quarters to form to a cone shape. Wrap in a clean kitchen towel to keep them soft and warm while you cook the others.

Eat warm.

# Beef Isthu

A MILD BEEF STEW

The existence of a mild "Western-style" stew in many regions of India is a reminder of our colonial history in South Asia. With the arrival of the wives of the East India Company officers in the seventeenth century, a style of Anglo-Indian cuisine developed where the cooks working in British households were trained to cook traditional British food, including the Sunday roast (see page 60). The cooks also learned to use Western cuts of meat when cooking, making stews and hybrid dishes, like kedgeree. In Kerala, they would add coconut milk to the stew, and you could add coconut milk to this recipe if you wanted to have a richer gravy. You could also swap the meat for goat or mutton, or use skinless, bone-in chicken thighs. In my home we would have this stew with boiled rice (see page 43).

2 tbsp plain flour

2 tsp salt

2¼lb (1kg) beef braising steak/ beef chuck/beef stew meat, cut into 2½-in (6-cm) pieces

4 tbsp vegetable oil

1¼ cup (350g) Spanish onion, thinly sliced into half-moons

1½lb (750g) new potatoes, scrubbed (or white potatoes, cut into 2-in/5-cm cubes)

½lb (300g) carrots, cut into 2-in (5-cm) pieces and halved if thick

1 heaped tbsp butter

1-in (2.5-cm) piece of fresh root ginger, peeled and grated, or ground to a paste

2½ cups (600ml) warm water

2 bay leaves

1 tsp whole black peppercorns

½ cup (150g) green peas (fresh or frozen)

1 cup (225ml) full-fat milk (or coconut milk)

In a bowl, season the flour with ½ teaspoon of the salt, add the meat pieces, and toss to coat with the flour.

Heat the oil in a heavy-based pan with a lid over a medium heat until it is shimmering. Add the sliced onions and stir-fry until they are dark brown and the edges are looking crispy. Be patient and keep stirring to ensure the onions are cooked evenly. Remove with a slotted spoon to a plate, and spread them out to cool and crisp up. Try to leave as much of the oil behind in the pan as possible.

Reheat the oil over a medium heat, add the potatoes, and fry until they are sealed and tinged brown. Remove with a slotted spoon to a plate. Repeat this with the carrots, and remove to the plate with the potatoes.

Add the butter to the remaining oil and let it melt, then add the meat and brown it in the fat. Add sprays of water if the meat is getting stuck to the pan. When the meat is browned, add the ginger and stir for a minute, then add the warm water followed by the bay leaves and peppercorns.

Crush the browned onions and return them to the pan with the remaining 1½ teaspoons of salt. Bring to the boil, then cover and reduce to a simmer for 30–40 minutes. The meat should be soft but not falling apart, ideally about three-quarters cooked. (If you are using chicken, the cooking time will need to be reduced by half.)

Bring the contents of the pan back to a rolling boil, then add the potatoes and carrots, cover, and simmer for another 20–30 minutes.

Check that the meat and vegetables are cooked. Once they are ready, remove the lid, add the peas, and bring to a boil. Reduce the heat and add the milk. Stir gently and taste for seasoning before serving.

# Tawa Toastie

The sandwich toaster or panini press is a valuable invention. I have one at home. I even have one at my restaurant. They offer the most practical way to make toasted sandwiches. But when I was growing up, toasties were made one of two ways: on a flat cast-iron *tawa* or in a flying-saucer–shaped sandwich iron that was held directly over an open flame. No toastie made in a machine comes close to these. It could just be nostalgia, but *tawa* toasties hold a special place in my heart. This sandwich can be cut into small triangles to be served as a canapé or cocktail snack. For the cheese, I use half Red Leicester and half mature Cheddar; Colby and sharp Cheddar will work too. Use whatever cheese you like—it just has to melt well!

½ cup (120g) salted butter, at room temperature

4 thick slices of white bread

3oz (80g) cheese of your choice, grated

1 tbsp finely chopped red onion

2 tbsp chopped fresh cilantro leaves

¼ tsp finely chopped green chiles, deseeded if wished *you may need more, according to how hot your chiles are*

2 tbsp *Hari Chatni* (cilantro chutney, see page 25)

4 tsp vegetable oil

Butter the bread on both sides. I prefer not to remove the crusts.

Mix the grated cheese with the chopped onion, cilantro, and chiles. Divide the cheese mixture into two parts.

Layer one side of each bread slice with a film of cilantro chutney. Carefully spread the cheese mixture on top of two of the slices (try not to add too much mixture at the sides as it may fall out and burn on the *tawa*) and sandwich with the chutney-spread side of the two remaining slices.

Heat 1 teaspoon of the oil on a *tawa* or flat skillet over a medium heat. Place a sandwich on the *tawa*, reduce the heat to medium-low, and cook, gently sliding the bread over the *tawa* to ensure the oil cooks the entire slice. Use a wooden spatula to press down on the sandwich. After 2–3 minutes it should be browned underneath. Turn with a metal spatula and cook the other side in the same way. You may need to add another teaspoon of oil. Keep the heat on medium-low to ensure that the cheese melts before the bread burns. When the sandwich is ready, take it off the *tawa* and serve with your favorite dipping sauce. I use tomato ketchup, but you can also just use more of your green chutney.

# ENDING ON A SWEET NOTE

### Match-Day Treat

This is a great combination of sweet dishes and a drink
to end a meal. It could be that the main meal is a pizza
delivery or takout, as everyone watches the game/match
on TV. These three dishes can be made in advance and
then served at the end of the day with minimum prep, to
celebrate or commiserate, depending on how the game
went! It also makes your guests feel you are indulging
them—a great way to end a day with friends and family.
The textures and flavors of all three are very different, but
they go really well together. The chile and chocolate in the
*barfi* is a perfect foil for the sweet banana pancake, and
both provide the perfect backdrop of sugar and heat for
the spiced, milky *karak chai.*

## MENU SUGGESTION

### Karak Chai
*Sweet*
PAGE 110

### Chile Chocolate Barfi
*Sweet*
PAGE 111

### Kolar Pitha
*Sweet*
PAGE 114

# Karak Chai

STRONG AND CREAMY SPICED CHAI

Despite the hot weather, the first thing I do every time I visit the Persian Gulf is have a hot cup of *karak chai* spiced black tea. *Chai-walas* from the Indian subcontinent traveled to the Middle East in the 1960s, bringing with them a tea culture that boomed in popularity. This drink is a great way to introduce yourself to the flavors of *desi chai. Karak chai* differs from traditional *masala chai* in that it typically contains fewer spices and is brewed for longer for a stronger flavor and thicker texture. In fact, *karak chai* simply translates to "strong tea." *Karak chai* is typically made with evaporated milk to achieve a creamier texture, but this recipe has directions for using fresh or evaporated milk. The recipe produces a basic *karak chai*, but you can experiment with adding peppercorns, ginger, star anise, cloves, and honey to your *chai* to add more breadth to its flavor profile. You can also experiment with using different kinds of tea leaves to get a range of different flavors.

3 tbsp white sugar, or more to taste

6 cups.(1.4 liters) water

4 tsp strong, loose-leaf tea or 4 tea bags *use something bold and robust like Orange Pekoe Assam, or a strong English Breakfast blend*

15 green cardamom pods, cracked

3-in (7.5-cm) cinnamon stick

1 cup (240ml) evaporated milk or 3 cups (750ml) full-fat milk (or milk substitute) *use unhomogenized milk if you want some malai or cream floating in your chai*

Add the sugar to a large saucepan set over a medium heat. Leave the sugar to melt undisturbed until it takes on an amber/caramel color.

Simultaneously, boil the measured water in your kettle. Carefully pour the hot water into the sugar pan, then add the tea and spices. Stir to combine and bring to a boil over a high heat.

If using evaporated milk, add it now, wait for the mixture to boil again, then reduce to a simmer. Stir with a ladle and aerate periodically by scooping a ladleful of *chai* out of the pot and pouring it back in from a few inches above. Start conservatively with this—as you get more comfortable with the movement, you can aerate from greater heights, which will result in a frothier texture. Simmer until your desired consistency and strength is achieved and serve hot. (This could be as little as 10 minutes; 30 minutes of simmering will produce a strong and creamy *chai*.)

If using regular milk, add it to the *chai* as above. Heat over a medium-high heat and bring to a rolling boil for 3 minutes. After this, allow the *chai* to boil to the brim on a high heat, then turn the heat down to allow the *chai* to settle. Repeat this process four times, or until you are satisfied with the consistency and strength.

Taste your *chai* and sweeten more if necessary. Strain into a teapot and serve hot.

*Pictured on pages 112–113*

# Chile Chocolate Barfi

*Barfi* is a fudge-like sweet usually made with slow-cooked milk flavored with essence/flowers/ spices, mixed with nuts, and cut into small, individual pieces. This recipe uses condensed milk, which reduces the cooking time. The combination of chile and chocolate gives this a distinctive flavor, but you can eliminate the chile if you wish. When this was made at home when I was a child, I would love to scrape the bottom of the condensed milk tin with a spoon and lick it!

4 tbsp (50g) ghee or
    unsalted butter
2 dried red chiles
1 x 14oz (396g) can sweetened
    condensed milk
3½oz (100g) unsweetened dark
    chocolate, grated
¾ cup (100g) cashew nuts/
    pecan nuts, chopped
¼ cup (50g) sugar

**EQUIPMENT**
10 x 10in (25 x 25cm) shallow
    pan/small baking dish,
    lined with greased
    parchment paper

Heat the ghee or butter in a heavy-based saucepan over a medium-low heat. Add the whole dried chiles and stir gently until they darken and release a smoky aroma. Use a slotted spoon to carefully remove the chiles, squeezing them against the inside of the pan to remove any excess fat. Place on a plate and leave to cool.

To the warm fat, add the condensed milk, grated chocolate, chopped nuts, and sugar, and stir. Reduce the heat to low and keep stirring until the contents start to come together, up to 15 minutes.

When the mixture comes together, transfer it to the lined pan/dish and spread out evenly. Use the back of a metal spoon to flatten the top. If you want to increase the chile flavor in the *barfi*, crush some of the cooled fried chiles and sprinkle on top of the warm mixture, but ensure you use just the bottom tip of the chillies and avoid using the seeds. Leave to cool and set before cutting into squares.

*Pictured on pages 112–113*

# Kolar Pitha

BANANA FRITTERS

This is a comforting, warm dessert of banana fritters, which I remember having with tea when I visited the homes of friends in Calcutta and Dhaka during monsoon season. In the sultry, humid monsoon weather, fruits like bananas would over-ripen very quickly. This recipe was a great way to use up ripe bananas, and the additional ingredients were staples that most people would have at home, so it did not require a visit to the bazaar in the rain!

4 large ripe bananas, about
   1¼–1⅓lb (500–600g), peeled
1½ cups (200g) plain flour
5 tbsp sugar (any type)
½ tsp ground cinnamon
¼ tsp salt
1 egg, beaten *optional*
1 cup (240ml) water
½ cup (120ml) vegetable
   oil, for frying

In a bowl, mash the bananas to a smooth paste using a fork.

Sift the flour into a separate bowl, then add the sugar, cinnamon, and salt, and mix with a wooden spoon to combine. If using, add the beaten egg followed by the mashed banana and stir well. Add the measured water in small quantities to make a batter that is of dropping consistency. Cover and set aside for 1 hour.

Heat the oil in a *karai* or wok over a medium heat. Drop tablespoon-sized amounts of the batter into the oil, then fry until golden, turning the fritters over to ensure they cook evenly. Use a slotted spoon to remove the fritters to drain on kitchen paper.

Serve hot. These fritters are great eaten on their own or with vanilla ice cream.

*Pictured on pages 112–113*

– Ending on a sweet note –

শরৎ

3

# SHÔROT

Fall

Fall is the season to slow down,
to take the time to nourish and heal both
body and soul. It's a moment to prepare for
the darker nights and colder mornings
ahead, embracing the changing rhythms
of life. While some regions see a riot
of reds and browns as the leaves turn, in
Bengal, the marigolds begin to bloom,
painting the landscape with cascades
of golden yellows and coppery oranges.
The air becomes cooler, and the pace
of life gentler, inviting us to reconnect with
ourselves and the earth.

In this season, ingredients like pumpkin
take center stage, offering a world
of possibilities. The Kadoo ka Raita
(page 138) and Pumpkin Dal (page 127)
showcase just how diverse and flavorful
seasonal produce can be, highlighting the
warmth and depth that fall cooking brings.
These comforting dishes are perfect for this
season of reflection, inviting you to savor
the flavors of fall while preparing for the
winter months ahead.

# Aloo
# Gosht Kalia

SLOW-COOKED MEAT AND POTATOES IN A THICK GRAVY

*Kalia* was the spicier, darker-gravied meat dish made by our family cooks in Calcutta.
We usually had this with plain boiled rice and a tangy salad, such as *Narangi* (page 207) or sliced
red onion marinated in lime juice, salt, and sugar. If you are making this for a large gathering
where guests will be standing to eat, it is best you use boneless beef or lamb, cut into 2-in (5-cm)
cubes. This is a great dish for boneless mutton as it can be slow-cooked to absorb all the spices
of the base gravy. Ensure the potatoes are not waxy, as the flavors won't permeate, nor
so floury that they easily crumble.

2 tbsp ginger paste

1 tbsp garlic paste

2 tsp red chili powder

1 tsp ground turmeric

1 tsp ground coriander

1 tsp roasted cumin powder
(store-bought or see
page 29)

2 tsp salt, or to taste

2¼lb (1kg) meat of choice, cut
into even-sized pieces
(see above)

¾ cup (175ml) vegetable oil

1 cup (200g) sliced white onions

4 medium potatoes (such as
Yukon Gold), halved

4 cloves

6 whole green cardamom pods

2 Indian bay leaves

2 x 2-in (5-cm) cassia bark
sticks (or cinnamon sticks)
*cassia bark has a deeper,
smoky, and more earthy
flavor, and works very well
with meat dishes like this*

4 cups (1 liter) warm water

chopped cilantro leaves and
sliced green chiles,
to garnish *optional*

In a large bowl, combine the ginger and garlic pastes, dried spices, and
salt. Add the meat and turn to coat in the marinade. Cover the bowl with
foil or a plate and set aside, but do not refrigerate.

In a heavy-based pan with a lid, warm the oil over a medium-high heat
until it starts to shimmer. Add the sliced onions and stir to ensure they
are browning evenly. Fry until a deep caramel brown color, then use a
slotted spoon to remove, and spread over a large plate to cool and crisp.
Leave as much of the oil as possible in the pan. Take the pan off the heat
while removing the onions, as there is a small chance that they may burn
if you do not work quickly enough.

Return the pan to a medium-high heat and wait for the oil to warm
back up. Add the potatoes and brown them on all sides. When they are
tinged with brown flecks, remove with a slotted spoon and set aside.
Do not fry them to a crisp.

To the remaining oil, add the whole spices, followed by the marinated
meat, and stir over a medium heat. If the meat is getting stuck on the
base of the pan, spray cold water on the inside edges of the pot and use
that moisture to deglaze the pan. Once the meat is browned on all sides,
slowly add the warm water and stir to ensure nothing is sticking. Crush
the browned onions in a pestle and mortar, add them to the pan, then
turn the heat up to high and stir for 5–8 minutes, until the contents are
boiling. Cover with a lid and reduce to a simmer. Occasionally stir and
check on the meat for doneness (the time this takes will vary, depending
on your chosen meat). You want the meat to be three-quarters cooked–
coming apart with some pressure but not yet falling apart. Once your
meat has reached this stage, add the potatoes back to the pan. Increase
the heat to high, bring back to a boil, then cover and simmer until the
meat and potatoes are cooked through.

Taste for seasoning and adjust, if needed. Serve over rice, garnished
with chopped cilantro leaves and green chiles, if wished.

# Shadha Bamdhakopi

## WHITE CABBAGE WITH TOMATOES AND CASHEW NUTS

My first encounter with white cabbage in England was at a college meal in Cambridge University–it was a shock! I was trying to make sense of the overcooked, sloppy vegetable in front of me. I just presumed cabbages in England were super soggy as it rained so much. I later learned it was just overenthusiastic boiling of the cabbage by the chef! The cabbage in this recipe should still have a bit of a crunch in it, and the addition of cashew nuts gives the dish a lovely texture.

4 tbsp vegetable oil

1 cup (150g) raw cashew nuts

2 dried red chiles

1 tsp cumin seeds

1 tsp ground turmeric

1 x 14oz (411g) can diced tomatoes (or 3–4 medium fresh tomatoes, chopped)

½ tsp chili powder

1½ tsp salt

1½lb (750g) white cabbage, shredded

2 tbsp chopped fresh dill (or any fresh herbs you have available), to garnish

Heat the oil in a *karai*, wok, or deep saucepan over a medium heat until shimmering. Add the cashew nuts and stir to ensure all sides are cooked. As they will continue to cook in the residual heat, do not wait until the nuts turn dark brown–turn the heat off and use a slotted spoon to remove them to a plate. Remove and discard any burned cashews as they will make your dish bitter. Try to leave as much of the oil behind in the pan.

Check there are no cashew pieces left in the oil and set the pan back over a medium heat. Once the oil is shimmering, add the whole dried chiles and cumin seeds, and stir until the chiles darken. Add the turmeric, then immediately add the chopped tomatoes followed by the chili powder and salt. Reduce the heat and keep stirring at regular intervals until the oil comes to the edges of the spiced tomato mix. With the heat on low, add the shredded cabbage and coat with the tomato mix. Increase the heat to medium-high. If the slices of cabbage are thin, stir-fry for 4–5 minutes. Thicker slices will need 6–8 minutes, covered, and a further 2 minutes of stir-frying uncovered.

Taste for seasoning, then return the cashew nuts to the pan and mix through. Garnish with the chopped herbs before serving.

This goes with any rice dish or bread. It is also the perfect texture to wrap in a chapati or tortilla, accompanied with a raita.

# WHEN THE NIGHTS GET LONGER

A Warming Fall Supper

The yellow curry is a recipe only made in my family. This is the taste of home. It is the perfect combination to cook when there is a change in seasons, as the long days and short nights come to an end and the chill of winter insinuates its presence, when you need to take out your warmer coat and put away your sandals. This yellow curry, rich with healing turmeric, and a nutritious dal are the boost that's needed with a backdrop of browning leaves and darker starts to the day.

## MENU SUGGESTION

**Ammu's Yellow Curry**
*Sweet*
PAGE 126

**Pumpkin Dal**
*Sweet*
PAGE 127

SERVE WITH PLAIN RICE

# Ammu's Yellow Curry

The yellow chicken curry is a dish only made in my mother's family. The source was the indomitable matriarch Begum Qamarunissa Khatun of Jalpaiguri, who created it as a mild healing "stew" for the children in the family. She headed the household, which included her seven sons and their families. This dish was created when the family lived in the sprawling Faiz palace in North Bengal and continued to be made when they moved to Calcutta in the 1940s. The yellow curry became the go-to for everyone needing a comforting dish, as well as a family staple. I remember sitting on the floor in the Rawdon Street balcony with my cousins, eating yellow curry and rice, watched over by "Dadu" when I was 5 years old—that was the last time I saw her. Her legacy lives on in her immune-boosting recipe.

4 tbsp vegetable oil
2 tbsp ghee
2 onions, finely minced
2 tbsp fresh ginger paste
1 tbsp garlic paste
½ tsp Kashmiri red chili powder
¼ tsp chili powder
1 tsp ground turmeric
4 tbsp full-fat plain yogurt
1½ tsp salt
6 medium bone-in chicken
   thighs, skin removed
warm water, as needed
1 cup (250ml) warm full-fat
   (whole) milk
4 fresh whole green chiles

Heat the oil and ghee, in a large pan that has a lid, over a medium-high heat. Add the minced onions and cook until they begin to caramelize, stirring continuously. Spray with water to deglaze the pan if the onions begin to stick. Add the ginger and garlic pastes and stir until the raw smell goes away, then add both kinds of chili powder, turmeric, yogurt, and salt, and cook for a few minutes until the turmeric becomes aromatic. The oil should separate and come to the edges of the pan.

Add the chicken and coat well, then add enough warm water to cover the chicken. Bring to a boil, then reduce to a low simmer, cover with a lid, and cook for 30 minutes. Check whether the chicken is cooked by taking a piece out, and use a knife to pierce through near the bone—it should not look red. When cooked, remove the lid and simmer over a high heat to reduce the gravy until it is thick and clinging to the chicken.

Finally, add the warm milk, then remove from the heat, add the fresh whole chiles, and gently stir before serving.

*Pictured on page 124*

# Pumpkin Dal

This is a great dish to make in the peak of the pumpkin season. With the nights getting longer and the temperature falling in parts of the western hemisphere, this dal is a great immune system booster with garlic and turmeric. The additional goodness of pumpkin makes this the perfect comforting food for a cold fall night. This dal can be eaten with rice or roti, or you could also have it on its own with a dollop of yogurt or crème fraîche. If pumpkin is not in season and you have any other leftover vegetable in your kitchen, use that instead. Cut the vegetable into small pieces and add to the dal. If you want to add spinach or kale, they would need to be added toward the end of the cooking process.

1 cup (200g) split red lentils
  (*masoor dal*)
4 tbsp vegetable oil
¼ cup (50g) onion, thinly sliced
1-in (2.5-cm) fresh root ginger,
  peeled and grated
5oz (150g) pumpkin (such as
  sugar/pie, Crown Prince,
  Delicata) chopped into
  1-in (2.5-cm) cubes
1 tsp ground turmeric
½ tsp chili powder
1½ tsp salt
4¼ cups (1 liter) water
1 tbsp tomato paste

FOR THE TEMPERING
2 tbsp ghee (or vegetable oil)
1 tsp cumin seeds
2 dried red chiles
4 garlic cloves, thinly sliced

Pick over the lentils for any impurities, then wash in several changes of cold water until the water runs clear. Soak the lentils for 30 minutes if you have time. Soaking will speed up the cooking process and will help to break down the dal when cooking, giving you a better texture. Unlike *channa dal* and *mung dal* that require soaking, *masoor dal* cooks quickly, so soaking is not absolutely essential here. Drain well.

Warm the oil, in a heavy-based pan that has a lid, over a medium heat. Add the sliced onions and stir until they start to turn brown, then add the ginger and keep stirring. Add the pumpkin along with the turmeric and chili powder, and stir for a minute, then add the salt and the drained lentils. Stir for a few more minutes, then add the measured water and bring to a boil. With a spoon, remove and discard any scum that may come to the top. Partially cover and reduce to a simmer for 30–40 minutes. Leave the lid slightly ajar—you need to keep stirring the dal at regular intervals.

When the dal and pumpkin are cooked, remove the lid, add the tomato paste, and stir to ensure it does not get stuck at the bottom of the pan. Take the dal off the heat. (At this point, you could cool the dal and store in the fridge until ready to eat, then reheat when needed.)

Temper the dal before serving. Heat the ghee in a small frying pan over a medium heat. Add the cumin seeds followed by the whole dried chiles and then the garlic. Keep stirring to ensure the garlic is cooked evenly. When the garlic is brown, tip the contents of the pan into the lentils. Taste for seasoning before serving.

*Pictured on page 124*

# Fish
# Kabab

Fish *kababs* are an impressive and unorthodox dish to serve at barbecues, the flavor and aroma of smoky fish is sublime. This dish is best cooked on a firepit or barbecue, therefore the choice of the skewer is very important when preparing this *kabab*. Ideally use thin metal skewers.

2¼lb (1kg) firm, skinless and boneless fish, cut into 1½-in (4-cm) cubes
3 tbsp ghee or melted browned butter (*beurre noisette*), for basting

**FIRST MARINADE**
1 tsp garlic paste
3 tbsp lime juice
3 tsp salt
2 tsp freshly ground black pepper

**SECOND MARINADE**
4 tsp mustard oil (or olive oil)
¾ cup (200g) full-fat plain yogurt
4 tsp garlic paste
2 tbsp finely chopped cilantro leaves or dill
4 fresh green chiles, finely chopped

**EQUIPMENT**
5–6 thin metal skewers

Combine the ingredients for the first marinade in a large bowl and mix until smooth. Add the fish and gently but thoroughly mix through the marinade to ensure the pieces are evenly covered. Leave to marinade in the fridge for 20–30 minutes.

Meanwhile, combine the ingredients for the second marinade in a separate bowl. Remove the fish pieces from the first marinade and add them to the second. The salt will have drawn moisture out of the fish, leaving a pool of excess liquid at the bottom of the first bowl—discard this, do not add

it to the second bowl. Cover the bowl and refrigerate for 4–5 hours.

Remove the fish around an hour before you intend to cook it, to allow it to come to room temperature. Skewer the fish on long, thin, metal skewers, leaving around ½in (1cm) between each cube of fish to allow the heat to cook the fish evenly. Preheat your barbecue until hot.

Cook the skewers on both sides over the hot barbecue. Once the color of the *kabab* begins to change—this may take between 8–10 minutes—start to baste with the melted ghee or browned butter. Ensure you wait for the *kabab* to be fully browned on the outside before basting, so the extra fat can properly do its job of adding a beautiful brown tinge and a subtle nutty flavor. Baste for around 3 minutes, or until the juices in the fish run clear. Serve immediately.

*Pictured with Beetroot and Moong Dal Chillah, page 130*

# Beet & Moong Dal Chillah

SAVORY LENTIL PANCAKES

*Chillah* are lentil pancakes, which can be made with black gram flour (*besan*) or split husked lentils like *moong*. This dish is often made at home and is also a popular street food in India. It is traditionally a breakfast dish, but can be eaten at any time of the day.

I have used *moong dal* in this recipe as it's a great way to get your family to eat more plant-based protein. If you really dislike beets, they can be swapped out for grated carrots. It's a great way to use up any straggling vegetables in your fridge—chopped beans, asparagus, broccoli or cabbage, cooked and squeezed chopped spinach, herbs, corn, or even crumbled paneer can be added to the lentil batter for added texture and nutrition.

As this pancake batter is gluten-free, it can make a great substitute for wheat-based flatbreads. You can make it in advance and reheat it for a barbecue or brunch, either on a dry pan over a low heat or wrapped in foil in a preheated low oven.

1½ cups (300g) *moong dal*
(yellow *mung dal*)
3¼ cups (800ml) water
for soaking, plus
4 tbsp for blending
⅓ cup (100g) finely chopped onion
¼lb (100g) fresh beets, finely
grated *or any vegetable of
your preference, finely grated
so they can cook at the same
time as the moong dal batter*
1-in (2.5-cm) piece of fresh
root ginger, peeled
and finely grated
1 tsp Kashmiri red chili powder
(or 1–2 minced fresh chiles)
*don't go overboard!*
2 tsp roasted cumin powder
(see page 29) *you can use
regular ground cumin but it
will lack the beautiful smoky
aroma of freshly roasted and
ground cumin*
1 tsp ground turmeric
1 tsp salt
2 tbsp chopped cilantro leaves
4 tbsp vegetable oil

Put the dal in a bowl and fill with cold water. Stir the dal gently by hand, then discard the water. Repeat this process until the water runs clear, then cover with the measured fresh water and leave to soak for at least 5 hours, or ideally overnight. The dal will slowly absorb the water and visibly swell after a few hours.

Drain the dal and wash it in cold water twice more. Drain again, then transfer the dal to a blender. Add the 4 tablespoons of cold water and blend until you get a smooth, thick batter. Do not be tempted to add more water! It's better to keep the batter thick at this stage. Only add extra water when blending if the batter is grainy and dry.

Transfer the dal batter to a bowl and whisk in the chopped onions, grated beets (or any vegetable substitute), grated ginger, chili powder or minced chiles (if using), cumin powder, turmeric, salt, and chopped cilantro. Cover and leave the batter to rest for 15 minutes. The addition of salt will result in the beets bleeding pink water into the batter, which will add a beautiful hue to your pancakes. Check the consistency and add more water, if needed—it should be the consistency of a thick pancake batter.

a ladle to both spoon out and
spread the batter *if you
don't have one, use a cup
for pouring and a flat spatula
to spread the batter over
the pan*

Warm a flat griddle or cast-iron pan over a medium heat. The pan must be hot before you add the batter to the pan, to avoid sticking. If using cast iron, a long preheat is vital. Over time, you will perfect how much batter to use for each pancake, but as an estimate it should be around 3–4 tablespoons (45–60ml)—you should get 15–18 *chillahs* from the batter. Drizzle ¼ teaspoon oil onto the warm pan, pour a ladle or cup of batter in the middle, and immediately spread the batter in concentric circles to make a pancake. The *chillah* should start to come away from the pan at the edges. Pour another ¼ teaspoon oil on the top of the pancake and turn it over with a spatula, pressing down on it with the back of the ladle or spatula to ensure the heat comes through. Remove when both sides are cooked with brown tinges. Repeat until all the batter is used up. The *chillah* can be served folded in half or into quarters in a cone shape.

*Pictured on page 128*

# PESCATARIAN LUNCH

## Two Meals in One

This combination of dishes can be eaten with rice or any kind of bread. I have even eaten this with heavily buttered, crisp toast! If you end up with leftovers, you can make a meal out them the next day by applying the chutney to bread and combining the potatoes and prawns or shrimp to make a Tawa Toastie (see page 106). The onions in the *do piaza* are a superfood, an allium, like garlic, which is good for your heart and helps with maintaining stable blood pressure. The contrast of flavors, textures, and colors in all three dishes is beautiful, as they combine in layers to stimulate the palate and provide a feast for the eyes and the tummy.

## MENU SUGGESTION

**Chingri Do Piaza**
*Sweet*
PAGE 134

**Aloo Dum**
*Pungent*
PAGE 135

**Dhania Pudina Chutney**
*Sweet*
PAGE 25

# Chingri Do Piaza

PRAWNS WITH DOUBLE ONIONS

This dish is quick to make with very few ingredients. Ideally it should be made with small, fresh prawns or shrimp. If you cannot get fresh prawns, you can substitute cooked frozen shrimp, which will impact the texture and aroma of the dish, but the flavors will still be there. *Do piaza* means "double onions," specifically double the onions that would normally be used in the dish. The onions are added in two different ways: crushed into a paste and also sliced. Red onions or shallots are preferred over brown or white onions, but this is pretty much a freestyle dish—you can play around with whatever you have to hand!

1lb (450g) onions: half roughly chopped; half thinly sliced into half-moons

1½-in (4-cm) piece of fresh root ginger, peeled

6 garlic cloves, peeled

4 tbsp vegetable oil

1 tsp ground turmeric

1 tsp ground coriander

½ tsp ground cumin

1 tsp salt

½ cup (120ml) warm water

2–2¼lb (900g–1kg) small/ medium raw prawns or shrimp, deveined and shelled

4 fresh green chiles, slit in the middle (if unavailable add 1 tsp chili powder)

1 tbsp lemon juice

2 tbsp chopped fresh cilantro leaves

In a food processor, blitz half the onions (the chopped onions) with the ginger and garlic.

Heat the oil in a *karai* or wok over a medium-high heat. Add the other half of the onions (the sliced onions) and stir until they are nicely caramelized. Add the onion paste followed by the ground spices and stir for a minute, then add the salt and warm water, and bring to the boil. Reduce the heat to medium and keep stirring until the water reduces and the raw smell of the garlic is gone. This may take 10 minutes. When the oil is visible around the edges of the onion mix, add the prawns and green chillies, and continue to stir until the prawns are pink and no longer translucent. (If you are using cooked prawns, just warm them through). Add the lemon juice and taste for seasoning.

Garnish with chopped fresh cilantro and serve with rice.

*Pictured on pages 136–137*

# Aloo Dum

FRIED BABY POTATOES IN A SPICY YOGURT

Aloo Dum and Lutchi (see page 246) is a classic Bengali combination, served by everyone from street cart vendors in the heart of Calcutta's commercial district to Sunday brunch at home. This is classic comfort food. A version of this kind of potato dish with a thick sauce exists from Kashmir to Kanyakumari (the southern tip of India). The small potatoes with their thick, clingy sauce make the perfect accompaniment to any meal. My perfect partnering would be with Choler Dal (see page 198), which is also a combination served in traditional Bengali wedding banquets.

1-1¼lb (500g) small
    new potatoes
2 tbsp ghee
1 tsp cumin seeds
5 bay leaves
1 tsp ginger paste
1 tsp chilli powder
1 tsp ground turmeric
1 tsp sugar (any type)
2 tbsp plain yogurt
1½ tsp salt
½ cup (120ml) water
pinch of asafoetida
½ tsp garam masala

Parboil the potatoes in their skins, then cool a little before removing the skins. Typically, in Indian cooking we skin the potatoes after cooking them, to avoid the potatoes absorbing too much water.

Pan-fry the potatoes in the ghee over a medium heat, along with the cumin and bay leaves, until the potatoes are golden brown and the spices are aromatic. Remove with a slotted spoon to a bowl.

Add the ginger, chili powder, turmeric, sugar, and yogurt to a separate bowl and stir to combine, then add the mixture to the potatoes. Stir in the salt and measured water, then stir in the asafoteida and garam masala.

Transfer the contents of the bowl back to the pan and reduce until the gravy clings to the potatoes.

Serve warm.

*Pictured on pages 136–137*

# Kadoo
# Ka Raita

### PUMPKIN WITH GARLIC YOGURT

The combination of pumpkin, garlic, roasted cumin seeds, and yogurt is one of my favorite combinations in a raita. The sourness of the yogurt is a great foil for the pungent garlic. Garlic is often called the destroyer of diseases, and this is a great fall dish to make to boost immunity before the cold winter months arrive.

1¼lb (800g) pumpkin (such as sugar/pie, Crown Prince, Delicata), peeled and chopped into 1-in (2.5-cm) cubes

4 large tomatoes, roughly chopped into 1-in (2.5-cm) pieces

1 large onion, roughly chopped into 1-in (2.5-cm) pieces

½ tsp chili flakes

2 tsp salt

3 tbsp vegetable oil

1 tsp cumin seeds

4 cups (1kg) full-fat thick plain yogurt

4 garlic cloves, finely chopped

½ tsp sugar (any type)

3 dried red chiles

fresh mint leaves, to garnish

Preheat the oven to 350°F (180°C).

Layer the pumpkin, tomatoes, and onion on a baking sheet. Sprinkle with the chili flakes and 1½ teaspoons of the salt and mix with 2 tablespoons of the oil. Bake in the oven for 30 minutes, stirring halfway. Check the pumpkin is fork tender but still firm. Leave to cool.

Dry-toast the cumin seeds in a skillet until they darken and begin to release a roasted, woody aroma. Transfer the cumin immediately to a plate to stop the cooking process. Crush the seeds in a pestle and mortar or in a spice grinder.

Put the yogurt in a bowl and add the chopped garlic, crushed cumin seeds, sugar, and remaining ½ teaspoon of salt. Whisk well.

Transfer the pumpkin mixture, including all the roasting juices, to a serving dish. Mix the spiced yogurt through the pumpkin mixture, then taste and adjust the seasoning.

The raita can be served at room temperature or chilled. Just before serving, heat the remaining 1 tablespoon of oil in a pan and add the dried red chiles. Do not break the chiles, as they will release all their seeds and make the tempering too spicy. Pour the chile tempering over the raita and serve immediately, garnished with fresh mint.

# SWEET DREAMS

A Weekend Treat

The base of *besan ka ladoo* is the flour of Bengal gram,
packed with protein, vitamins, and minerals like iron,
which gives the *ladoo* a uniquely rustic flavor and texture.
They pair perfectly with the milky and soothing Kashmiri
*chai*. All of us have those sweet cravings—mine are usually
late in the evening on a weekend. You do not need to eat
dry cereal out of the box or open a packet of cookies
thinking you will eat a few and end up eating the lot
(although there is nothing wrong with this!) if you have
these to hand. *Besan ka ladoo* keep well and can
be stored for three weeks (or refrigerated for up to three
months) and are easier to enjoy in moderation compared
to the saccharine vices just mentioned! Pink *chai* takes
a bit of time to make but is a beautiful, indulgent,
Eastern alternative to hot chocolate!

MENU SUGGESTION

**Besan Ka Ladoo**
*Sweet*
PAGE 142

**Kashmiri Noon Chai**
*Salty*
PAGE 143

# Besan Ka Ladoo

SWEET BENGAL GRAM FLOUR LADOOS

Synonymous with celebration and jubilation, the *ladoo* has made its way into Indian adages
of happiness, victory, and celebration. "*Dono hathon mein ladoo hona*," literally meaning to have a *ladoo*
in both hands, means to be in a win-win situation. "*Man mein ladoo phutna*," meaning to be overcome
with euphoria, translates literally as an eruption of *ladoo* in the mind. *Ladoos* truly are bundles of joy.
*Besan ka ladoos* are probably my favorite kind of *ladoos*, the nuttiness of gram flour and crumbly texture
make for a symphonic layering of flavors and textures befitting of the *ladoo*'s delightful reputation. You
can use white granulated or caster (superfine) sugar for this recipe, but I like the aroma of brown sugar
as it reminds me of unrefined *shakar* sugar that was used to make these *ladoos*
in my father's ancestral home.

1 cup (200g) demerara, brown,
or unrefined sugar

6½ tbsp (100g) ghee

⅓ cup (50g) unsalted nuts (a
mix or just one type: shelled
pistachios, cashew nuts,
or almonds)

1½ cups (200g) coarse
gram flour (*besan*)

good pinch of freshly grated
nutmeg or crushed
cardamom seeds *pick
one—do not add both!*

Grind the sugar in a blender to a fine powder. Set aside.

Take a deep, heavy-based cast-iron saucepan (it should have a diameter
of over 10in/25cm). Heat 2 tablespoons of the ghee over a medium-low heat,
then add the nuts and slowly stir-fry until you see tinges of brown on the
outside. Do not cook the nuts beyond this point. If the heat is too high,
the outsides will roast, but the insides will still be raw. Use a slotted spoon
to remove the nuts to a plate (not paper towels) to cool and harden. Once
the nuts are cool, crush or chop them into smaller pieces, as you prefer.

Add the gram flour to the remaining ghee in the pan and continue
to roast over a low-medium heat. Use a wooden spoon with a flat edge
to stir, as you need to scrape the flour at the bottom of the pan. If you
feel the flour is darkening immediately and getting stuck at the edges, the
pan is too hot. Remove from the heat and continue to stir—once the flour
is not getting stuck at the edges, put the pan back over the heat and keep
stirring. The flour will start to darken and release a beautiful nutty aroma
(see tip). Be patient and continue roasting—this must be done slowly and
carefully to ensure that all the flour is roasted and it no longer smells
raw. This can take 4–8 minutes.

Next, add the remaining ghee to the pan and continue roasting. Keep
stirring for a further 10–12 minutes, until all the ghee seems to have
disappeared. Turn off the heat and continue to stir. After 3–4 minutes,
add the powdered sugar, nutmeg or cardamom, and the crushed/chopped
nuts. Keep stirring until all the sugar has melted. The mixture may seem
runny at this point, but be patient—it will harden as it cools. Taste and
check whether it is sweet enough—you can add more sugar if you want
at this stage and stir until it dissolves.

Once the mixture is cool enough to touch and has hardened, divide it
into six portions and roll them between your hands to form smooth balls.
These can be stored in an airtight container for up to a week.

TIP   If you are new to roasting gram flour, keep some unroasted flour
on a small plate nearby. By smelling the unroasted flour, you will know
when the flour in the pan is roasted by the nutty aroma!

*Pictured on pages 140*

# Kashmiri Noon Chai

### PINK CHAI WITH STAR ANISE AND CRUSHED NUTS

Kashmiri *noon chai* is a fascinating recipe. It originated in the Kashmir valley and its history is contested, as many have argued that the rose-hued tea has its roots in the infamous Silk Road. Comparisons have been drawn between *noon chai* and the salty yak-butter tea of Tibet (which relies on a similar chemical reaction to achieve its color) and the salty milk teas of Central Asia. Today, this drink is staunchly Kashmiri—a breakfast staple that is enjoyed with bread and biscuits. *Noon* means "salt," alluding to the fact that this is a salty tea. Because of this, it pairs well with my sweet Saffron and Poppy Seed Kulcha (see page 203). It develops its striking hue when baking soda is added to a very strong green tea decoction. This produces a rich, burgundy-colored liquid, which takes on its distinctive pink coloration when brewed with milk and aerated. Kashmiri *noon chai* leaves can be hard to find, but gunpowder green tea works well too for its rich and intense flavor.

**FOR THE DECOCTION**
2 cups (500ml) room-
　temperature water
10 green cardamom pods,
　cracked open
2-in (5-cm) cinnamon stick
1 star anise
3 tbsp green tea leaves
　*gunpowder tea leaves are*
　*best, or use the freshest*
　*green tea leaves available*
½ tbsp baking soda
¼ tsp Himalayan pink salt
5 cups (1.25 liters) ice-cold
　water

**TO SERVE (PER 2 CUPS)**
1½ cups (350ml) full-fat
　milk of choice
　*unhomogenized or*
　*gold-top milk will give*
　*you a creamy finish*
2 tsp sugar (any type)
crushed pistachios and
　almonds, to garnish

In a large saucepan, bring the room-temperature water to a boil over a high heat. Make sure the pan is less than halfway full. Add the spices, bring back to a boil, then add the green tea. When the tea reaches a rolling boil, add the baking soda. The mixture will fizz. When the tea settles, add the pink salt and stir. Reduce the heat to medium and simmer, aerating it with a whisk until the volume of water has more than halved to less than 1 cup. In between bouts of whisking, use a large ladle to aerate the *chai* by lifting a ladleful out and pouring it back into the pot from a height. If the *chai* reaches the top of the pot, reduce the heat to let it settle, then return to a medium-high heat.

Once the tea has reduced, add 2 cups (500ml) of the ice-cold water to the pan. Reduce as before until the volume has more than halved, stirring and aerating continuously.

Once this has reduced, add the remaining ice-cold water to the pan and follow the same process, stopping when you have 2 cups (500ml) of liquid in total. Check that the tea leaves are very soft–this means they have released all their flavor. Strain into a deep bowl and whisk thoroughly for 2 minutes. You can either use a hand whisk or get a second bowl and pour the mixture back and forth from a height. This improves the color and flavor. It is fully aerated when it turns from burgundy to a crimson color. Pour the decoction into a sealable container. It will keep for around 1 week in the fridge.

To serve, heat the milk and sugar in a small pan. Stir and aerate the milk while you bring it to a boil over a medium-high heat. Add ½ cup (120ml) of the decoction to the milk and bring back to a boil. Divide between 2 cups and serve garnished with crushed nuts.

*Pictured on pages 140*

হেমন্ত

◇ 4 ◇

# HEMONTO

Dry season

The dry season in Bengal brings a shift in the air. The humidity lifts, nights become clearer, and a cool breeze begins to sweep through, marking a time of excitement and anticipation. There's a palpable buzz as households prepare for Durga Puja, a festival that celebrates the homecoming of the goddess and her victory over evil. It's a time of joy, reunion, and spiritual reflection.

This season also brings with it an abundance of nutrient-rich leafy greens, such as fenugreek. These greens, when paired with mustard seeds, lend a characteristic bitterness to many traditional dishes like Shukto (page 163). The flavors of this time of year are distinct—earthy, slightly sharp, yet deeply satisfying. For those willing to experiment, cooking with these ingredients offers unparalleled depth, inviting you to explore the unique and rich culinary traditions that accompany this sacred time of year.

# Tamarind Prawns

This dish needs to be made with raw shelled prawns or shrimp. I usually make this dish using tiger prawns, but you can use any kind of prawn or shrimp. Whatever size you choose, be mindful that you do not overcook them. Prawns or shrimp will continue to cook in their residual heat, so do not cook them until they are done all the way through. Take them off the heat when they are three-quarters done and stir to finish the cooking. This way, they will stay succulent. This is a tangy, spicy dish that is ideally served with rice. Avoid using ready-made tamarind concentrate for this dish. Most South and East Asian grocery stores will have dried tamarind pulp. If you must use concentrate from a jar, add it sparingly and taste before adding more.

2-in (5-cm) square piece of dried, seedless tamarind pulp

1¾lb–2lb (800–900g) raw shelled prawns or shrimp (about 30–36 medium tiger prawns)

2 tsp ground turmeric

4–6 tbsp coconut oil or vegetable oil

1¾ cup (180g) white onions, thinly sliced into half-moons

1 tsp fennel seeds

4 dried red chiles

2 tbsp ginger paste

1 tbsp garlic paste

1 tsp chili powder

1 tbsp ground coriander

1 tsp ground cumin

good pinch of sugar

salt, to taste

2 tbsp grated fresh coconut, to garnish *optional*

Soak the tamarind in a cup of warm water for at least 30 minutes. Occasionally rub the tamarind to ensure the water is penetrating.

Place the prawns or shrimp on a plate and rub with ¾ teaspoon salt and 1 teaspoon of the turmeric. Set aside for 20 minutes.

Meanwhile, heat 4 tablespoons of oil in a deep saucepan over a medium-high heat until shimmering. Add the onions and fry, stirring frequently, until golden brown. Once the onions look golden, carefully remove with a slotted spoon and spread on a plate to cool. Make sure you remove all the onions, as small pieces left behind will burn and make the gravy taste bitter. Once the onions are cooled, grind them to a paste in a blender and set aside. If the oil left in the saucepan looks like less than you may need, add a further 2 tablespoons (if in doubt, add more oil, as excess oil will separate from the gravy and can be left behind when serving). Bring the oil back up to shimmering, and add the fennel seeds followed by the dried red chiles. Stir for a minute until the chiles darken, then add the ginger and garlic pastes and stir for a couple of minutes. If anything is sticking, spray with cold water to deglaze the pan. Once the aroma of raw garlic is gone, add the remaining turmeric, chili powder, ground coriander, and cumin. Stir for a minute until the turmeric loses its raw aroma, then add the raw prawns (leave behind any of the liquid that will have collected on the plate), and stir to coat with the spices. Cook over a medium-high heat for 2 minutes, then add the onion paste and keep stirring for a few minutes until all the prawns are pink.

Strain the tamarind pulp through a sieve and add to the pan with a pinch of sugar. Stir, then remove from the heat. Taste for seasoning. Garnish with the fresh grated coconut and serve.

If you do not plan to eat the prawns immediately, and do not want the heat and flavors of the chillies to intensify, remove all the whole red chillies now and set aside. When you want to serve the prawns, flash fry them in the same pan and serve on top of the chiles.

# DATE NIGHT

Tangy Textures

Let me start with the *missi roti*. If you wear the chef's
pants in your relationship, you can get your less culinarily
inclined partner to help with the roti, which can be made
just before you eat. There is no deep-frying or dextrous
folding involved in making this bread. A perfectly round
roti is overrated anyway—anything roundish is acceptable!
This will be an excellent test of their true character—will
they indulge you or are they so insecure that they will not
try doing something new? The combination of these
breads with the vinegar-flavored *sirka gosht* and crunchy,
poppy seed potatoes is the perfect meal.

MENU SUGGESTION

**Sirka Gosht**
SOUR
PAGE 153

**Bengali Aloo Posto**
*Pungent*
PAGE 154

**Missi Roti**
*Spicy*
PAGE 156

# Sirka Gosht

### SLOW-COOKED LAMB WITH VINEGAR

One of the most well-known dishes using vinegar is a Goan dish, *vindaloo,* which is based on the Portuguese dish *carne de vinha d'alhos.* I am not sure why a bastardized version of this dish became a staple on all the menus in British curry houses! Vinegar production is very regional in India and it is made in fascinating ways, such as by putting iron nails into a pot of sugar-cane juice to ferment. The vinegar we would use for this dish in Calcutta was made with *jamun* (black plum), and the distinctive, fruity, tart flavor of the fruit is still etched in my memory. During the summer holidays, we would eat the berries sitting under the shade of the tree in our garden. If you can find a fruity vinegar to add to this dish, it will make a difference to the flavor.

4 tbsp vegetable oil

2-in (5-cm) cassia bark (or cinnamon stick)

3 cloves

3 green cardamom pods

1 Indian bay leaf

1 dried red chile

2¼lb (1kg) boneless lamb, cubed
*if you can get your butcher to cut leg or shoulders into pieces, the flavor will be enhanced by the inclusion of the bones*

2 small onions, finely chopped, then crushed to a paste

4 garlic cloves, crushed to a paste

1 tbsp fresh ginger paste

1 fresh green chile, slit lengthways

½ tsp ground turmeric

1½ tsp ground coriander

1½ tsp ground cumin

1 tomato, diced

1½ tsp salt

2¾ cups (700ml) water

4 tbsp fruity-flavored vinegar, or to taste

In a heavy-based pan that has a lid, heat the oil over a medium–high heat. Add the cassia bark, cloves, cardamom pods, bay leaf, and dried red chile. Stir until the spices and the chile have darkened in color. Using a slotted spoon, remove the whole spices and chile from the pan to a plate and set aside.

In the same pan, fry the meat in the chile-infused oil until brown on all sides. Do not allow the meat to cook through; the aim is just to brown the meat. Remove the meat from the pan to the plate with the fried spices and set aside, leaving as much of the oil in the pan as possible.

Add the onion, and garlic and ginger pastes to the pan (take care as the pastes will sputter in the hot oil), along with the green chile. Next, add the ground spices, then add the diced tomato and fry for 2 minutes before returning the fried whole spices, dried chile, and browned meat to the pan. Add the salt, measured water, and vinegar, bring to a boil, then cover the pan with the lid and reduce to a low simmer. It is always better to cover the pan while it is boiling and then lower it to simmer, as this traps more of the heat in. Simmer for 1½ hours.

Once the meat is cooked, remove the lid, and reduce any remaining liquid until the oil seeps to the edges of the pan. Usually, I add some extra vinegar at this stage, too—it depends on whether the vinegar aroma was lost in the cooking process. Taste and adjust to your liking.

Serve with bread or rice.

# Bengali Aloo Posto

POTATOES WITH POPPY SEEDS

For decades I ate this dish without understanding the poignant symbolism of the poppy seeds in it. In Bengal, there are many dishes in which poppy seeds are used. Once I understood why, I was moved by the ingenuity of the home cook–the woman who found ways to nourish her family. Preceding the Opium Wars with China in the nineteenth century, the colonial forces in India started forcing farmers to grow opium, which was sent to China in exchange for tea. The price paid for the crop was severely regulated, and often the farmer was left with hardly any money after selling the crop to feed his family. The only thing left was the seeds of the poppy harvest. The farmer's wives started to add the poppy seeds to the limited food they could afford, to bulk it up and give their families something more substantial to eat. I cook this dish in honor of all the women who, in every generation and in every challenging time, have found ways to nourish their families.

1½ lb (700g) new potatoes *any waxy potato will work*

¼ cup (50g) white poppy seeds, soaked in water overnight or for a minimum of 3 hours, then drained

1 tbsp ginger paste

2 green chiles

¾ cup (200g) plain yogurt

5 tbsp ghee or vegetable oil

1-in (2.5-cm) cassia bark (or cinnamon stick)

½ tsp nigella seeds

1 Indian bay leaf

½ tsp ground turmeric

1 tsp salt

3 tbsp lemon juice

2 tbsp chopped fresh cilantro leaves, to garnish

Boil the potatoes until fork tender, then remove the skins and cut into 1-in (2.5-cm) cubes. The actual shape of the potatoes does not matter–it is more important that they are all the same size. If the potatoes are cut too small, there is a risk that they will break. If they are too big, the spices and flavors will not penetrate through.

In a blender, blitz together the poppy seeds, ginger paste, green chiles, and yogurt to a smooth paste. Coat the potatoes with the spiced yogurt paste, cover, and leave to marinate in the refrigerator for at least 1 hour.

When you are ready to cook, allow the potatoes to come up to room temperature.

Heat the ghee or oil in a *karai* or deep saucepan over a medium-high heat. Add the cassia bark, nigella seeds, and bay leaf, and stir for a minute. When the nigella seeds are sizzling, add the potatoes in their marinade along with the turmeric and salt. Stir to coat the potatoes evenly. When the potatoes are starting to get tinged with brown specks, reduce the heat and continue to cook until the potatoes look dry and crusted with the marinade. Add the lemon juice before serving, garnished with cilantro leaves.

# Missi Roti

This roti is made with a combination of two types of flour: gram flour (*besan*) and wholewheat chapati flour (*atta*). The yellow *besan* is often called chickpea flour—but it is not made with the tan-colored, large chickpeas we call *kabuli channa* in Hindi. *Besan* is made with *kala channa*, black/dark brown chickpeas, which are the native chickpeas of India. The skins of the chickpeas are removed and the yellow seeds are ground to a smooth powder. *Missi roti* is made in many regions of North India, from Rajasthan to Punjab. I enjoy the texture of the onions and the nuttiness of the flour in this bread. I personally love to have this roti with plain yogurt and pickle.

1 tsp fresh root ginger, peeled and grated

2 tbsp chopped fresh cilantro leaves

2 green chiles, chopped *do not use bird's-eye chiles as they will make the roti too spicy*

2¾ cups (350g) gram flour (*besan*), plus extra for dusting

1½ cups (200g) wholewheat flour

1 tsp ground turmeric

1 tsp salt

¾ cup (200ml) warm water

½ tsp dried chili (red pepper) flakes *optional*

¼ cup (60g) red onions, finely chopped *avoid large Spanish/white onions, which are too wet*

2 tbsp vegetable oil (or ghee or unsalted butter), for cooking

In a food processor, mince the ginger, cilantro leaves, and fresh chiles, then add both the flours followed by the turmeric and salt. Start adding the water slowly, with the motor running, and wait for the dough to gather into a rough ball. It is important to trickle the water in, as you need to make a firm but pliable dough. Pouring in too much will make a dough that is too sticky.

Transfer the ball of dough to a lightly floured work surface. Add the chili flakes and chopped onions, and knead into the dough with your knuckles. Add more flour, if required (it can be one type of flour or a mix of both flours). Gram flour tends to be stickier, so if the dough is too wet add more wholewheat flour. Once you have a dough that feels soft and pliant, transfer to a bowl and cover with a damp cloth or plastic wrap, and set aside for 1–2 hours.

Warm a *tawa*, cast-iron griddle, or frying pan over a medium heat.

Once the dough has rested for 30 minutes, divide it into 12 equal balls. Cover the remaining balls as you start to make the roti. On a floured work surface, roll a ball of dough into a circle, 6in (15cm) in diameter. Transfer to the hot pan and let it cook for 1–2 minutes, then carefully turn the roti and cook on the other side for 1–2 minutes. Brush the side you cooked first with oil, then turn over and press down with a wooden spatula to ensure the heat is penetrating through the roti. Repeat the process of brushing oil on the dry side of the roti and turn to cook that side too. This should be quick, as you want to ensure even cooking and brown speckles on the roti—you do not want to burn it!

Wrap the cooked rotis in a clean kitchen towel and serve together. You can also make the rotis in advance, separate each one with parchment paper, seal with foil, and refrigerate. The roti can be reheated over a low heat when ready to eat.

*Pictured on page 155*

# Eggplant
# with Poppy Seeds

Eggplant is called *brinjal* in India, or *baingan* in Hindi, and is often referred
to as a "poor man's crop," as it was grown in India by farmers with small land holdings. This
is a vegetable that was native to the Indian subcontinent and was used extensively throughout the
country. The small individual farming tradition of *brinjals* has often meant a variety of different
shapes and sizes. This recipe is a combination of poppy seeds and eggplant–an uncommon
partnering which nevertheless works well.

1½ lb (750g) eggplant, unpeeled,
cut into 1½-in (4-cm) cubes *if
using baby eggplant, remove
the stalk and cut them in half*

½ tsp chili powder

½ tsp ground turmeric

1 tsp salt

1½ tbsp white poppy seeds,
soaked in water for
30 minutes, then drained

3 fresh green chiles, chopped

4 tbsp vegetable oil,
or as needed

2 dried red chiles

1 bay leaf

1 tsp cumin seeds

1 tsp nigella seeds

4 garlic cloves, minced

3 tomatoes, chopped

½ tsp sugar

1 cup (240ml) water

Place the eggplant cubes on a plate and sprinkle with the chili powder,
ground turmeric, and ½ teaspoon of the salt. Rub well to ensure all the
pieces are covered and set aside for 20 minutes. (Adding salt serves
2 functions: it adds umami and reduces moisture, which in turn reduces
the amount of oil the eggplant will absorb when frying. Avoid keeping the
marinated eggplant in a bowl, as the moisture draining out from the top
layer will seep into the pieces below it.)

Grind the soaked poppy seeds and chopped chiles to a paste in a pestle
and mortar. Set aside.

Squeeze the eggplant pieces gently to remove excess water, and discard
any liquid that has collected on the plate.

Heat the oil, in a deep, heavy-based pan that has a lid, over a medium
heat until shimmering. Fry the eggplant cubes, until each piece is tinged
with brown. Use a slotted spoon to remove the eggplant pieces and spread
on paper towels.

Ideally, you should have 1½–2 tablespoons of oil left in the pan–add
more if not. Reheat to medium-high, add the dried red chiles and bay leaf,
followed by the cumin and nigella seeds. Stir-fry for 30 seconds, add the
minced garlic and stir-fry for a few seconds, then add the chopped
tomatoes. Use the liquid from the tomatoes to deglaze the pan and release
any garlic pieces that may have got stuck to the bottom. Add the poppy
seed paste along with the sugar and the remaining ½ teaspoon of salt.
Add the water and continue to cook uncovered over a medium-low heat
for 3–4 minutes, until the liquid has reduced somewhat. Return the
eggplant to the pan and coat with the spice paste. Bring to a boil, then
cover and reduce to a simmer for 5–7 minutes. Do not stir the eggplant
at this stage except to release any spice paste from getting stuck to the
bottom–you do not want to mash the eggplant. Remove the lid and
increase the heat to medium-high, until the oil comes to the edges of
the pan. Taste for seasoning and adjust.

# OH CALCUTTA!

A Taste of Bengal

This is probably the favorite meal combination in most Bengali households. The fresh flavors of seasonal vegetables in *shukto*, and bitter undertones from the addition of bitter gourd and bitter spices, is the best contrast to the vibrant fish curry. Traditionally, the fish we used in my home in Calcutta was the fresh river fish rohu, which had a delicate, sweet flavor. Other river fish, such as carp and bream, are good alternatives. If you prepare the rice using the draining method, it enhances the flavors further, as the rice seems to absorb the gravy of the fish much better. This is on my list of the top meals of my childhood in India!

MENU SUGGESTION

**Bengali Fish Curry**
*Sweet*
PAGE 162

**Shukto**
*Bitter*
PAGE 163

# Bengali Fish Curry

Calcutta's location on the banks of the Hoogly River, a tributary of the mighty Ganges River, means it has always been a city to which traders came from around the world with goods, and in which some stayed behind. This gave the city a tradition of diverse food. This dish, however, is purely Bengali! A healing, simple fish curry made with the freshest fish, landed at dawn at the fish markets of the city. The best way to enjoy this dish is with boiled rice (see page 42). The one thing I taught both my sons from a young age was how to eat fish curry and rice with their hands, so they could feel the thin fish bones by touch. This is definitely one dish worth eating with your hands!

1½ tsp ground turmeric

1½ tsp salt

2¼lb (1kg), about 6 fillets, firm, white fish (carp, barramundi, black cod)

4 tbsp vegetable oil

1lb (450g) white potatoes, cut into 2-in (5-cm) cubes *do not use floury potatoes as they will crumble*

2 tbsp ghee

4 bay leaves

2 green cardamom pods

2 cloves

1-in (2.5-cm) cassia bark (or cinnamon stick)

3 medium white onions, thinly sliced into half-moons

2 tsp garlic paste

2 tbsp ginger paste

4 tbsp ground onion paste

1 tsp chili powder

3 cups (750ml) warm water

1 green chile *optional*

pinch of sugar

Rub half of the ground turmeric and a good pinch of the salt over the fish fillets and set aside for 20 minutes. Discard the water that is released from the fish and pat the fillets dry with paper towels before frying.

Heat the vegetable oil in a deep heavy-based pan that has a lid, over a medium-high heat. Fry to brown the fish fillets on both sides. Do not cook the fish all the way through. Remove the fish to a plate.

To the same oil, add the potato cubes and cook until tinged with brown on the outside edges, then remove to a plate.

Add the ghee to the remaining oil and bring it back shimmering over a medium-high heat. Add the bay leaves, cardamom pods, cloves, and cassia bark. Stir until the spices darken, then add the sliced onions and fry until they become a caramel color. Add the garlic and ginger pastes, followed by the onion paste, and the remaining turmeric, salt, and chili powder. Stir well and if anything is sticking, spray with water to deglaze the pan. Add the measured water along with the potatoes, and bring to a boil, then cover and reduce to a simmer. Check on the potatoes after 10 minutes, then frequently until they are almost cooked through. Taste the gravy and a small piece of potato to check the seasoning, and adjust the salt to taste. In Bengal, we do not add a lot of chiles to our food, but you can break a green chile in half, and add it to the gravy at this stage if you want more heat.

When the potatoes are almost cooked, remove the lid and increase the heat to medium–high. Stir until most of the liquid in the pan has reduced. Add a good pinch of sugar and stir until it dissolves, then gently add the fish fillets back to the pan and coat with the gravy. Reduce to a simmer for a few minutes, until the fish is cooked through, and the gravy has thickened.

*Pictured on pages 164–165*

# Shukto

## TRADITIONAL BENGALI STIR-FRIED VEGETABLES

In some families, this Bengali dish would have added "*bari*" (drops of sun-dried lentil paste) or a handful of soaked black gram. These were not added by my family and I am sharing the recipe as I remember it. This dish is traditionally eaten at Bengali feasts at the start of the meal. The bitter vegetables in the *shukto* were meant to act as a stimulant to activate the palate to prepare for the richer and often protracted meal that lay ahead.

1 medium potato
1 bitter gourd (this can be
   omitted or replaced with
   any other gourd)
2 small zucchini
3½oz (100g) drumsticks or
   French beans/green beans
   (drumsticks are a long, thin
   green vegetable)
1 green plantain
¼ cup (50g) peas
¼lb (100g) cauliflower florets
1 tsp poppy seeds
½ tsp mustard seeds
2 tbsp mustard oil
   (or vegetable oil)
½ tsp panch phoran
   *if unavailable, use a*
   *mix of fennel seeds,*
   *fenugreek seeds, and*
   *black mustard seeds*
1 tbsp fresh root ginger, peeled
   and finely grated
1½ cups (350ml) water
1 tbsp grated fresh coconut
   *optional*
1½ tsp salt
½ tsp sugar
2 tbsp ghee
2 fresh green chiles, halved

Wash and cut all the vegetables into ½-in (1-cm) pieces. If using drumsticks or beans, cut them to a little over 2in (5cm) in length to ensure they do not break and disintegrate in the cooking process.

Grind the poppy seeds and mustard seeds in a spice grinder to a fine powder. Set aside.

If using mustard oil, heat the oil to smoking point to get rid of some of its pungency, then reduce the heat to medium. This is not necessary if you are using vegetable oil. Add the panch phoran. Once the mustard seeds start to pop, add the ginger and stir until it starts to get a brown tinge. Add all the vegetables and stir for a minute, then add the measured water. Scrape up any bits that have stuck to the pan, then add the poppy and mustard powder along with the coconut (if using). Keep stirring the vegetables for another minute, then add the salt and sugar. Reduce the heat and let the vegetables simmer uncovered. As the gravy thickens, add the ghee and green chiles, and continue to simmer slowly until the excess moisture in the gravy has evaporated. Taste for seasoning and adjust.

Serve with boiled rice.

*Pictured on pages 164–165*

# Haldi Dood

## MILK INFUSED WITH TURMERIC AND GINGER

Before turmeric lattes were à la mode, *haldi dood* was the South Asian household's healing elixir of choice. This drink can help reduce inflammation and boost immunity through the potent curcumin present in turmeric, and can soothe and warm during the cold winter months with its comforting and slightly spiced flavor. To get the most out of this drink I recommend adding the black pepper, as this is supposed to help with the absorption of curcumin. If you cannot have milk, make sure to find an alternative way to add some fat to this drink, as curcumin is fat soluble. Using fresh spices is, in my opinion, better tasting and better for you, but it can leave you at a risk of curdling your milk. You will still get all the nutritional benefits of *haldi dood* if you prefer to use dried spices.

12½ cups (3 liters) full-fat milk of choice

6 tbsp grated fresh turmeric root (or 1½ tsp ground turmeric)

2 tbsp fresh root ginger, peeled and grated *optional*

1½ tsp freshly ground black pepper *optional*

18 green cardamom pods, crushed *optional*

1 cup (240ml) honey (local honey, if you can, or use maple syrup or agave), or to taste

Boil the milk over a medium heat, stirring with a ladle, and aerating frequently by scooping up a ladleful and pouring it back into the pan from the height of a few inches. Once boiling, add the turmeric, ginger, black pepper, and cardamom pods (if using). Bring back to a rolling boil, stirring and aerating constantly to guarantee a frothy texture. Strain and serve hot, sweetening each cup with honey to taste.

# HIGH CHAI

Tea Time

When you turn up to an Indian home at teatime,
you may be surprised at what accompanies the *chai*
(see recipes on pages 00, 00 and 00). The least you will
be offered is cookies and some local version of *channa
chur*/*chewda*/Bombay mix. If you are lucky (and give your
hosts enough notice to prepare before your arrival), you
will be presented with a spread like this.

As my mother had a catering business, we would
always have uneven offcuts of fish in the kitchen,
as we would buy whole fish for our clients and use the
leftover pieces to make meals for staff, family, and
friends. These offcuts are perfect for fried fish dishes that
make a great centerpiece for an Indian teatime spread. We
would usually serve this crispy fish with a couple of other
savory options, usually sandwiches or pakora, and
a sweet dish, usually semolina *halwa*, as it was quick
and inexpensive to make, with ingredients that we often
had to hand! Pictured opposite is the drawing room from
my own family home in Aligarh.

MENU SUGGESTION

**Calcutta Fish Fry**
*Pungent*
PAGE 170

**Sooji Ka Halwa**
*Sweet*
PAGE 171

SERVE WITH CHAI
*(I have used Kashmiri Noon Chai, page 000)*

# Calcutta Fish Fry

This is a dish unique to Calcutta (Kolkata), and a real celebration of the culinary heritage of the city. As a significant trading port in the east of the Indian subcontinent, Calcutta was at the crossroads of a myriad of food cultures. The marination of the fish in a base of herbs and chiles is similar in many ways to the Parsi *patra ni machhi*. The coating of the fish in breadcrumbs is possibly an ode to the British influence in Calcutta, which was for many decades the capital of the British Empire in India.

¼ cup (60g) Spanish onion, coarsely chopped

2½-in (6-cm) fresh root ginger, peeled

6 garlic cloves, peeled

3 green chiles (deseeded if hot)

2 tbsp roughly chopped fresh cilantro

1 tbsp roughly chopped mint leaves

2 tbsp lime juice

¼ tsp sugar

2 tsp salt, plus an extra pinch for the breadcrumbs

1 tbsp freshly ground black pepper

6 square-shaped white fish fillets (barramundi, bekti, tilapia, cod, or basa), about 5oz/140g per fillet

½ cup (75g) plain flour

2 large eggs

fine breadcrumbs, for coating

vegetable oil, for deep-frying

Place the onion, ginger, garlic, green chiles, cilantro, and mint in a blender and blitz to a smooth paste (you may need to add a little water to help it along). Transfer to a bowl, stir in the lime juice, sugar, salt, and half of the black pepper.

Place the fish fillets in a sealable container, pour the marinade paste over the fillets, and ensure that they are well covered. Cover and refrigerate for 2 hours.

Dust the work surface and a plate with the flour. Remove the fish fillets one at a time from their container (do not allow excess liquid to stick to the fish), coat in the flour, and place on the plate. Break the eggs directly into the container with the leftover marinade, and whisk to combine. Pour the breadcrumbs onto a separate plate, add a generous pinch of salt and the remaining black pepper, and mix well. Dip the fish fillets first into the egg mixture, then transfer to the breadcrumbs and coat on both sides. Use one hand for dipping the fish in the egg mixture and the other to cover with the breadcrumbs. Flatten the fillet and shape with a butter knife to a square shape. The edges have to be smooth. Once each fillet has been shaped, cover and refrigerate for 1 hour.

Heat enough oil for deep-frying in a deep pan over a medium heat. Fry the fillets to golden brown, about 3 minutes on each side.

Traditionally, this fish fry is served with a dipping sauce of Bengali mustard (*kasundi*). Dijon mustard is an alternative. I also like to dip the fish fry into Thai sweet chili sauce.

*Pictured on pages 172–173*

# Sooji Ka Halwa

SEMOLINA HALWA

Semolina *halwa* is made for many festivals and auspicious days in India, from Shab-e-Baraat to Ganesh Chaturthi. It is a great dessert to make for large gatherings, as it can be made in advance and reheated before serving. The ingredients are inexpensive and it does not take long to make. The addition of nuts is traditional, but you can remove them if required. To make the *halwa* vegan, you could use high-quality cold-pressed coconut oil instead of ghee, and replace the milk with your favorite milk substitute. I love this *halwa* warm and recommend that's how you serve it. You could also pour the warm *halwa* into a tray with buttered parchment paper, let it cool and set, then cut into squares.

2½ cups (650ml) full-fat milk, water, or milk substitute
2 green cardamom pods
7 tbsp (100g) ghee
1 cup (150g) semolina
10 raw cashew nuts
¾ cup (150g) white or brown sugar
2 tbsp toasted slivered almonds

EQUIPMENT
a deep, heavy-based pan that distributes heat evenly, such as a cast-iron Dutch oven

In a milk pan or deep saucepan, warm the milk over a low heat. Bash the cardamom pods with the side of a knife to split the pods open, and add to the milk. Stir occasionally to prevent sticking.

Separately, heat the ghee in the heavy-based pan over a medium heat. Once the ghee has melted, add the semolina and cashew nuts, and stir continuously to ensure they do not burn and are being cooked evenly. The roasting process can take 6–8 minutes. You will know it's done when the semolina begins changing to a darker shade and the cashew nuts brown. This is an important stage, as inadequately roasted semolina will not make great *halwa*, because it will lack the deep fudgy aroma needed. It will also make the texture gritty. If for any reason you burn the semolina, start again. You cannot do anything to rectify burned semolina.

When the semolina looks evenly roasted (at this stage the ghee will also start sputtering and coming to the edge), increase the temperature under the milk pan to high. Remove the semolina from the heat and gently pour the hot milk into the semolina pan. The mixture will sputter—the best way to prevent getting any splashes on your hand is to stir using a wooden spoon with a long handle. Stir the mixture well to prevent any lumps.

Return the semolina mixture to a medium-low heat and keep stirring to help it absorb the milk. When the mixture looks like it is bubbling up, add the sugar and continue to stir. Reduce the heat if you feel the mixture may be burning. Add the toasted almond slivers and continue to stir. The *halwa* is ready to serve when the mixture starts to leave the edges of the pan and comes together in the middle.

If you are not eating the *halwa* immediately, let cool, cover, and refrigerate. Reheat gently in a nonstick pan until the ghee is glistening on top, then serve.

*Pictured on pages 172–173*

শীত

⟨5⟩

# SHEET

Winter

Winter in Bengal marks the beginning of the wedding season, a time filled with excitement and joy. I remember sitting with the women in my family, applying henna in intricate patterns, and gathering outdoors to cook over open fires. The chill in the air was punctuated by visits to bustling night markets for last-minute wedding shopping, where the energy was infectious and the streets were alive with color. The weather is crisp, the nights misty, and the smoky scent of wood fires lingers in the air.

The food of winter is a perfect reflection of the season, divided between hearty winter warmers like Sardiyon ka Shorba (page 212) and the rich, celebratory cuisine of weddings, such as Biyer Bari Roast (page 182). These dishes offer a comforting warmth and richness, perfect for both the cold weather and the festive spirit. Some of my all-time favorite recipes are found in this chapter, inspired by the flavors and memories of winter.

# Karai Gosht

SPICED LAMB

This dish of spiced lamb is named after the utensil in which it is cooked. A *karai* is similar in shape to a wok and was traditionally constructed of cast iron. *Karai gosht* was something made in my home on special occasions such as weddings, usually in the colder months when we all craved spicy meat dishes. The flavor is enhanced from using meat on the bone. We usually ate this with roti or paratha. If you do not have a *karai*, you can substitute it with a cast-iron pot—using a thinner pot can easily lead to burning. In this recipe, the meat needs to be stir-fried slowly, to reduce the liquid to the point where the sauce is almost dry and clinging to the meat.

½ cup (120ml) vegetable oil

2 Indian bay leaves

2-in (5-cm) cassia bark, broken into pieces

4 dried red chiles

3¼lb (1.5kg) boneless lamb or mutton, cut into 1½-in (4-cm) cubes (if the meat is bone-in, cut into 2-in/5-cm pieces)

2½ cups (750g) white onions, finely chopped

1 tbsp garlic paste

2 tbsp ginger paste

½ tsp dried fenugreek leaves

½ tsp ground turmeric

1 tsp chili powder

1 tsp Kashmiri red chili powder (or smoked paprika or cayenne pepper)

1 tbsp ground coriander

1 tsp ground cumin

2¼lb (1kg) fresh tomatoes, diced or 2 x 14oz cans (822g) diced tomatoes

2 tsp salt, or to taste

2 cups (500g) full-fat Greek yogurt

2 cups (500ml) warm water

½ tsp sugar (any type)

slivers of fresh ginger, to garnish

fresh green chiles, slit in the middle, to garnish *optional*

Heat the oil in your *karai* or cast-iron pot over a medium heat until shimmering (it may seem like a lot of oil, but most will separate from the meat after cooking and you can remove it before serving). Add the bay leaves, cassia bark, and dried red chiles, and stir. Once the chiles have darkened, add the meat and stir until browned on all sides. Reduce the heat to low and use a slotted spoon to remove all the meat and spices to a large plate, leaving behind as much of the oil as possible.

Reheat the oil over a medium heat and add the onions. Stir for a couple of minutes until translucent, then add the garlic and ginger pastes and continue to stir until the raw aroma of the garlic is reduced. Add the dried fenugreek leaves, turmeric, chili powders, ground coriander, and cumin, and stir for a few seconds. Add the chopped tomatoes and salt, increase the heat to medium-high, and continue to stir and loosen any spices that are stuck to the pan.

When you can see the tomatoes breaking down, add the meat and spices back to the pan and stir. Add the yogurt a few tablespoons at a time, so the water in the yogurt has a chance to evaporate. Once all the yogurt has cooked through, add the warm water and bring to a boil. Cover and simmer over a low heat for about 30 minutes. Take a piece of meat from the middle of the pan and place on a plate to check for doneness. It should be three-quarters cooked—the meat should be pliant but not soft.

Remove the lid from the pan and bring the contents to a rolling boil. Keep stirring to prevent the meat or spices from sticking and add the sugar. You want the meat to have a thick gravy clinging to it, reducing the liquid until the meat has a glazed look. Taste for seasoning and add more salt if required. Before serving, garnish with slivers of fresh ginger and the chiles, if wished.

# Biyer Bari Roast

WEDDING CHICKEN

This is a roast chicken, but not as you know it. This classic chicken dish is served at weddings in Bangladesh. *Biyer bari* in Bengali literally means "wedding home." Traditionally the chicken is served as a quarter–the full leg. The base of the thick, clingy gravy is formed by the juice of the chicken bones. As long as you use some or all of the chicken leg to make this dish, you will get a delicious, glossy gravy for the chicken. If you have a large, heavy-based pot, like a Dutch oven, which will fit the full legs, then you can make this recipe in the traditional way. Using just the thighs also works well if you don't have a big-enough pan. This is one of those dishes that tastes better the next day. If you are cooking this for a party, you can make it the day before, cool, and store it covered in the fridge.

⅓ cup (50g) raw cashew nuts

¼ cup (25g) raw almonds

2 tbsp (20g) white poppy seeds

1½ cups (350ml) hot (not boiling) water

6 tbsp (85g) ghee

½ cup (150g) white onions, thinly sliced into half-moons, plus ⅓ cup (100g) finely chopped

2½-in (6-cm) fresh root ginger, peeled and roughly chopped

8 garlic cloves, roughly chopped

2 tsp salt, or to taste

½ cup (120g) full-fat plain yogurt

3 tbsp Kashmiri chili powder

4 tbsp vegetable oil

4 Indian bay leaves

2 dried red chiles

6 medium, skinless, chicken-leg quarters (leg and thigh) (or 3¼lb/1.5kg bone-in thighs, skin removed)

1½ tbsp sugar (any type)

1 tsp kewra water *optional*

edible gold or silver leaf, to garnish *optional*

Put the nuts and poppy seeds in a heatproof bowl, cover with ½ cup (120ml) of the hot water, and set aside.

Preheat a cast-iron or heavy-based skillet over a medium-low heat, then dry-roast the masala spices for 1–2 minutes, stirring frequently to ensure they do not burn and are roasted evenly. Transfer to a plate and let cool. When cool, grind the spices to a powder in a spice grinder. Depending on your grinder, you may end up with a stubborn piece of cassia bark that will not grind. I simply add it to the oil when sealing the chicken pieces.

Warm the ghee in a heavy-based pot or Dutch oven over a medium heat until shimmering. Add the thinly sliced onions and stir until they are golden brown. Turn the heat off, then use a slotted spoon to remove all the fried onions to a plate. Try to remove every piece of onion and leave behind as much of the ghee as possible (strain if you find there are too many small pieces of onion). Separate the onions with a fork so they become crisp as they cool.

In a blender, combine the ginger, garlic, finely chopped onion, half of the fried onions, salt, yogurt, and Kashmiri chili powder. Grind to a paste. Transfer to a bowl and rinse the blender cup.

Drain the nuts and poppy seeds, reserving the soaking water. Rub the skins off the nuts and discard. Add the nuts to the blender along with the poppy seeds and blend, incrementally adding the reserved soaking water until you have a smooth paste.

Reheat the remaining ghee along with the vegetable oil until shimmering. Add the bay leaves, dried red chiles, and any unground pieces of cassia bark (or cinnamon). Stir for a few seconds, then add the chicken pieces and brown them until speckled with brown. You do not want to fry to a crisp golden brown, just brown the pieces so there is no visible pink. If you have the time, frying in batches of no more than a couple of pieces at a time is ideal. Use a slotted spoon to remove the chicken pieces and spices to a plate.

**MASALA**

5 tbsp coriander seeds

1 tbsp cumin seeds

1½-in (4-cm) cassia bark
(or cinnamon stick),
broken into small pieces

2 large mace blades

¼ piece of a small nutmeg,
grated or broken into small
pieces (or 1½ tsp grated)

7 cloves

Add the onion paste and the masala powder and stir over a medium-high heat for a couple of minutes. Add another ½ cup (120ml) of the hot water to loosen any stuck pieces and prevent the paste from burning. Once the oil comes to the edges of the pan, return the chicken to the pan and stir to coat well. Add the nut and poppy seed paste along with the sugar, and continue to stir to ensure all the chicken pieces are well coated. Increase the heat to high, add the remaining hot water, and bring to the boil, then cover and reduce to a simmer. Cook for 20–25 minutes until the chicken is soft but not falling apart, and the edges are curling. Check to see whether the juices in the chicken are now running clear; if they are not, simmer for a further 5–10 minutes. When the juices are running clear, break off a piece to taste for seasoning.

If using, sprinkle the kewra water over the chicken (to add a touch of floral sweetness) and garnish with the remaining fried onions.

If you are cooking this the day before, leave the onion garnish uncovered in a bowl to use the next day. Use the kewra only after you have reheated the chicken. To reheat, allow the chicken to come to room temperature and preheat the oven to 375°F (190°C). Wrap the chicken and its juices tightly in foil and bake for 15–20 minutes. Carefully remove the foil and continue to bake for a further 15 minutes. Check the chicken is piping hot throughout before serving, garnished with edible gold or silver leaf (if wished).

*Pictured on pages 182–183*

# WINTER FUEL

## Warming Supper for a Cold Night

The aromas from the *kabab* and the *naan* as they cook
will envelop your kitchen with smoky umami fragrance—
the perfect fragrance on a cold evening. *Naan* and *kabab*
are a classic combination, which you can find versions
of from Central Asia to North Africa. Wherever you are,
there are probably easier and more convenient ways
to order these in or buy them, but I would really
recommend trying to make your own at least once!
Combined with a wintery cranberry chutney, which gives
the meal a pungent/tangy accompaniment, this meal feels
like a warm hug.

MENU SUGGESTION

**Dahi Murgh Kabab**
*Pungent*
PAGE 186

**Karonda Aur Khajur Ki Chutney**
*Sour*
PAGE 190

**Tawa Naan**
*Salty*
PAGE 191

# Dahi Murgh Kabab

YOGURT-MARINATED CHICKEN KABAB

Winter is wedding season in India. The logistics of entertaining large crowds are made so much easier by cold weather, as both the cooking and the dining can be done outdoors. *Dahi murgh kabab* was one of our regular family wedding dishes served on a large platter with wedges of *gondhoraj lebu* (the aromatic Bengali lime). This is a tangy dish and the additional zip of a citrus of your choice adds vibrance and dimensionality to the flavors of the dish. This easy and flavorsome yogurt-marinated chicken kebab makes a great addition to your barbecue repertoire and it can also be cooked in an oven. The recipe works best with skinless, bone-in chicken legs, but you can always experiment and use the same marinade and method to cook other meats. The marinating process is very important, so please keep the additional time in mind. The yogurt in the second marinade also needs to be hung, which can be done while marinating the chicken in the first marinade. Any leftovers can be cooled and refrigerated. The next day, the chicken can be shredded and used in salads or sandwiches.

6 medium chicken-leg quarters (leg and thigh), skin removed, (about 3¼lb/1.5kg)
melted ghee, for basting
lime wedges, to serve

**FOR THE FIRST MARINADE**
3 tbsp fresh lime juice
1 tsp Kashmiri red chili powder
2 tsp salt

**FOR THE SECOND MARINADE**
1¼ cups (300g) hung yogurt (see page 71)
2 tbsp ginger paste
1 tbsp garlic paste
1 tbsp garam masala (see page 32 for homemade)
1 tsp dried fenugreek leaves
2 tsp Himalayan rock salt (or 1½ tsp salt)
1 tsp Kashmiri chili powder
1 tsp brown sugar

Score both sides of the chicken legs with a sharp knife to help the marinade penetrate the meat. Do not make deep incisions, as this may result in the chicken falling off the bone during cooking.

Mix the first marinade ingredients together in a bowl and rub evenly over the chicken. Transfer the chicken to a flat, sealable container, cover tightly, and refrigerate for 1 hour, turning the pieces over halfway through. Marinating the chicken in a deep bowl is not ideal as the marinade does not spread evenly and often pools at the bottom.

Combine the second marinade ingredients, pour into the chicken container, and spread evenly with your hands. Cover and refrigerate for at least 6 hours, but ideally overnight.

Bring the chicken to room temperature before cooking.

If you are grilling the chicken on a barbecue grill, cook the chicken over a medium heat, on a mesh or grill set at least 4in (10cm) away from the direct heat. To make your life easier (especially if you're cooking for a large group and/or managing other dishes at the same time), thread a couple of the legs on a metal skewer so you can turn two legs at a time. Baste with melted ghee and cook for at least 5–6 minutes on each side, or until the juices run clear when the legs are pierced.

If you are cooking in an oven, preheat the oven to 350°F (180°C).

Place the chicken legs on a baking sheet, cover with foil, and bake for 40 minutes. Halfway through, remove the foil, baste the chicken with ghee, and turn each piece around, then re-cover with foil and return to the oven.

After 40 minutes, remove the foil and bake uncovered for a final 10–15 minutes until the juices run clear. Baste the chicken a couple of times with ghee during this final stage.

Serve with lime wedges, bread, and sweet-and-sour chutney (see page 190).

*Pictured on pages 188–189*

# Karonda Aur Khajur Ki Chutney

CRANBERRY AND DATE CHUTNEY

This cranberry and date chutney has a *khatta meetha* (sweet and sour) flavor profile. It goes well with roasted meats—even your Thanksgiving or Christmas turkey—and will add a zingy, tangy element to your meals, as well as healthy compounds like pantothenic acid, which helps to convert the food we eat into energy. Most botanical berries are good for you, as they contain antioxidants and a broad spectrum of vitamins and minerals. Making a chutney with berries will give you an easily accessible source of goodness beyond the short berry season, wherever you live. Feel free to swap the cranberries for any local berries you might have.

1½ cups (350ml) water
2 dried red chiles (optional, or reduce to 1 chile if you want to make it milder)
4 green cardamom pods
3-in (7.5-cm) cinnamon stick
1 tsp whole cloves
3½oz (100g) pitted dates, chopped
1½ cups (300g) brown sugar
1lb (450g) cranberries (fresh or frozen)

Bring the measured water to a boil in a small pan. Add all the spices to the boiling water. Do not break the dried chiles (if using) as they will release all their seeds and make the water far too spicy. After 1 minute, reduce to a low simmer for 15 minutes. Do not cover.

Strain the mixture to remove all the spices, return the water to the pan, and bring it back to a boil. Add the dates and brown sugar, and let it boil for 1 minute, then reduce to a simmer for 10 minutes.

Add the cranberries and continue to cook on a low simmer for another 10 minutes.

Serve at room temperature. Store extra chutney in sterilized jars in the fridge. Make sure to use a dry spoon to take out the contents, as moisture can dramatically shorten the shelf life of your chutney. A carefully jarred chutney should keep for a few weeks in the fridge.

*Pictured on pages 188–189*

# Tawa Naan

*Naans* are traditionally cooked in a *tandoor* or a clay oven and are not usually made at home. The logistics do not make it economically viable for a small family, as the amount of coal or wood necessary to get a clay oven hot enough to make bread makes it hard to justify anything other than a very large batch. The reason almost all Indian restaurants offer *naan* is because they have a *tandoor* on full heat and can quickly slap some dough in the oven to make a bread for service! This recipe is for a homemade version, which can be cooked on a griddle or *tawa*, then finished under a hot broiler. It can also be shaped on a baking sheet and baked in the oven for a larger group.

¾ cup (200g) plain yogurt

2 eggs

4½ cups (600g) plain flour

1½ tsp baking powder

1 tsp sugar (any type)

1½ tsp salt

¾ cup (175ml) water

4 tbsp melted (but not hot) ghee, plus extra for basting

1–2 tbsp vegetable oil, for greasing

2 tbsp milk, for brushing

1 tbsp nigella seeds, for sprinkling (or sesame or poppy seeds)

Whisk the yogurt and eggs separately and set aside.

Sift the flour into a bowl and add the baking powder, sugar, and salt. Mix well, then add the whisked yogurt and eggs, and mix gently. Add the measured water gradually and knead to form a soft, pliant dough. Do not overwork the dough—it should form a soft and slightly sticky ball. Use half of the melted ghee to grease the bowl, and swirl the dough ball in it so it is evenly covered in a thin layer of ghee. Pour over the remaining ghee and rub on top of the ball of dough. Cover with a damp cloth and set aside for 20 minutes.

Heat a *tawa* or cast-iron griddle over a medium heat, ensuring it is evenly hot. Preheat the broiler to high, and prepare a baking sheet on which you can place the *naan* and put it under the broiler.

Tear the dough into 8 even-sized balls. Roll the balls in the ghee that was used to grease the bowl. Keep the remaining balls covered in the bowl as you work on each *naan*. If the *naan* is not being eaten immediately, prepare a basket or container lined with a clean kitchen towel and cut 8 pieces of parchment paper to separate each naan.

Rub vegetable oil on a smooth surface or chopping board so the *naans* don't stick. Increase the heat of the *tawa*/griddle to high and start to work on the first *naan*. Using your fingers to stretch the ball, either shape the dough into a 5 x 7-in (12 x 18-cm) long teardrop shape, or roll the ball into a 5-in (12-cm) circle. Use your fingers or a pastry brush to brush a thin film of milk over the rolled *naan* and sprinkle with nigella seeds. Transfer the *naan* to the hot, dry *tawa*/griddle—it will puff up in just over 1 minute. Carefully transfer the *naan* to the baking sheet, and place it under the broiler until it gets some brown spots on top.

Serve immediately or transfer to your prepared container, interleaving each *naan* with a piece of parchment paper to prevent it from sticking, and cover with the kitchen towel. To reheat, warm in a low oven, or on an iron griddle or *tawa* over a low heat.

If you are oven-baking the *naan*, preheat the oven to 475°F (240°C) and heat a foil-lined baking sheet inside. Shape the *naans*, brush with milk and a sprinkling of nigella seeds, and bake for 2–3 minutes until the bread is puffed up. Serve immediately or store and reheat in a low oven before serving.

*Pictured on pages 188–189*

# Gobi Manchurian

STIR-FRIED SPICY CAULIFLOWER

There is nothing Manchurian about this dish, it was a name invented to give the impression that this was a dish of Chinese origin. The claim to inventing this dish has been attributed to a Calcutta-born chef, Nelson Wang, who created this dish in 1975 at the Mumbai Cricket Club, when requested to make a new dish that was not on the menu. There are of course other claims, attributed to Indian street stalls that sold noodles and a variety of Chinese dishes to hungry office-goers. The flavors in this dish are unique, and it goes well with plain egg noodles or boiled rice.

1lb (450g) cauliflower, cut into medium-sized florets

salt, as needed

vegetable oil, for deep-frying

**FOR THE SAUCE**

3 tbsp vegetable oil

2 dried red chiles

4 shallots or small red onions, chopped into chunks

2 tbsp crushed garlic

1 tbsp fresh root ginger, peeled and grated

3 tbsp dark soy sauce

3 tbsp tomato ketchup

2 tbsp white wine vinegar

2 tsp sugar (any type)

2 tsp chili powder

1 tsp ground white pepper

½ cup (120ml) water

**FOR THE BATTER**

5 tbsp plain flour

4 tbsp cornstarch

1 tbsp garlic paste

1½ tsp ginger paste

½ tsp salt

¼ tsp freshly ground black pepper

water, as needed

Heat the oil for the sauce in a *karai* or wok over a medium-high heat until shimmering. Add the dried red chiles (break the chiles to release their seeds if you like the dish spicier) followed by the chopped shallots or onions, and stir-fry. Once the shallots are translucent, add the garlic, ginger, soy sauce, ketchup, vinegar, sugar, chili powder, and white pepper. Stir for a few minutes, then add the measured water, bring to a boil, then reduce the heat, and let the sauce simmer and reduce until the top looks shiny.

Meanwhile, blanch the cauliflower florets in salted water for 10 minutes. Drain and cool under cold running water to stop the cooking process. Dry the florets on paper towels.

Heat a 2-in (5-cm) depth of oil in a frying pan over a very low heat.

Mix all the batter ingredients together, adding enough water to make a thin batter, the consistency of heavy cream. Add the cauliflower florets and turn to coat in the batter.

Increase the heat under the pan to medium, and fry the cauliflower florets in batches of 4–5, so they cook evenly and are crisp. Drain the fried florets on paper towels.

Once all the florets are fried, add them to the sauce, ensuring they are all well covered, and serve immediately.

You can make this in advance, but the cauliflower will no longer be crunchy. It will still be a wonderfully spicy, pungent, and tongue-tingling dish.

# Jali Kabab

## LAMB KABAB

This lamb *kabab* is a very traditional dish served at weddings in my family, particularly those hosted by the Dhaka side of the family. *Jali* means "web" or "mesh" in Bengali and describes the distinctive design on top of the meat patty created by the egg wash, which resembled the threadlike web pattern of a *jali*. Great to make for entertaining, *jali kabab* is also suitable for gatherings with children or adults with low chile tolerance, as you can halve the chile here without compromising much on flavor.

2¼lb (1kg) ground lamb (or other meat, under 10% fat)
2 tbsp tomato ketchup
1½ tsp soy sauce
1½ tsp chili powder
1 tbsp finely minced garlic
1 tbsp fresh root ginger, peeled and finely minced
½ tsp salt
½ tsp freshly ground black pepper
1 cup (100g) fine breadcrumbs
6 eggs
3 slices of white bread (if required)
vegetable oil, for deep-frying

**FOR THE ROASTED KABAB MASALA**

1 blade of mace (½ tsp ground mace can be substituted)
2 green cardamom pods
1-in (2.5-cm) cassia bark (or cinnamon stick)
2 cloves

Roast the kabab masala spices in a dry pan until they lose their raw flavor. Transfer to a spice grinder and blitz to a fine powder (discard any large pieces of mace or cassia bark). Making freshly roasted and ground kabab spice for this dish will make a difference to the taste. You can, if required, substitute the masala with 1 teaspoon of garam masala.

In a large bowl, mix the lamb with the tomato ketchup, soy sauce, chili powder, garlic, ginger, salt, pepper, kabab masala, and breadcrumbs. Break three of the eggs into a separate bowl and whisk, then add the eggs to the meat mixture and mix well. If the mixture is not binding, you can soak the extra bread in water, squeeze well, then crumble and mix it in thoroughly. You should only add one slice of bread at a time, as that might be enough. The moisture in store-bought ground meat to that made fresh by a butcher or at home can vary a lot, which is why the additional bread may be required to bind the *kabab* together. The mixture should feel like a mix for a burger. Divide the mixture into 12 portions and flatten into patties. Chill in the fridge for at least 30 minutes.

Whisk the three remaining eggs. Remove the *kababs* from the fridge.

Warm a deep, heavy-based frying pan over a medium-high heat, before adding a 1½-in (4-cm) depth of vegetable oil. When it reaches a medium-high heat (one way to test this is to drop in a small cube of bread—it should brown in 30 seconds), dip a *kabab* into the beaten eggs and slide into the oil. Ideally, you should fry no more than 2–3 *kababs* at a time. Adding too many will drop the temperature of the oil and cause the *kabab* to disintegrate during cooking. Wait for each *kabab* to brown and cook on one side before turning them over. With a pastry brush dipped in the beaten egg, drizzle a threadlike zigzag pattern on each *kabab*. Cook on both sides until each *kabab* is dark brown and cooked all the way through. Reduce the heat under the pan if the *kababs* brown too quickly—the insides must cook too. Remove with a slotted spoon to rest on paper towels.

Serve warm.

# WEEKEND LUNCH

## A Plant-Based Meal

Eating more plant-based food should never feel like
a chore. *Choler dal* is a thick, protein-packed, flavorsome
Bengali lentil, which is served in homes in Bengal on
weekends with what feels like unending quantities of
freshly made breads. The addition of *aloo gobi bhaji* brings
a nice texture to the meal and breaks the monotony of
creamy lentils and bread, and the turmeric in the dal and
the spices in the *bhaji* are all great for the immune system.
It makes a perfect weekend lunch.

### MENU SUGGESTION

**Choler Dal**
*Sweet*
PAGE 198

**Aloo Gobi Bhaji**
*Spicy*
PAGE 202

**Saffron and Poppy Seed Kulcha**
*Sweet*
PAGE 203

# Choler Dal

BENGALI CHANNA DAL WITH COCONUT

There is something very special about this *channa dal* with coconut. In Bengal, almost every meal with rice had a lentil accompaniment. For us, *bhaat dal* (rice and dal) is equivalent to bread and butter–they almost always go together. However, this dal is not that everyday accompaniment, which is usually made with red lentils or *moong dal*. *Choler dal* is typically served on special occasions, such as a wedding or a festival. It is not a soupy dal that is eaten with rice, as the texture is thick, enriched with coconut, and so usually eaten with *Lutchi* (Bengali fried bread, page 246).

Although this is not an everyday dal, it is remarkably easy to make. The only challenge is buying the right lentil. *Channa dal* is the yellow interior of the split, skinless black chickpea–Bengal gram. It should not be confused with yellow split peas, which look similar but are a different lentil–*tuvar dal*. Buying pulses and lentils at Indian grocery stores can be bewildering at first, do not hesitate to ask for help!

Traditionally, this dal has a hint of sweetness, which gives it its distinctive flavor. A great way to balance the flavors of a meal is to serve this with a vegetable dish, such as Aloo Posto (page 154) or Shukto (page 163).

1½ cups (250g) *channa dal*
4–5 cups (1–1.2 liters) cold water
1½ tsp ground turmeric
2-in (5-cm) cinnamon stick
  (or cassia bark, but do not
  use ground cinnamon)
2 cloves
2 whole green cardamom pods
1 large or 2 medium
  Indian bay leaves
2 tsp salt, or to taste
2 tbsp ghee (or vegetable oil)
1 tbsp raisins

Wash the dal as you would rice, rinsing with cold water until the water runs clear. I prefer to soak the washed dal in cold water overnight. Less soaking time will mean a longer cooking time for the dal.

Drain the dal and add to a large heavy-based pan that has a tight-fitting lid. Add 4 cups (1 liter) of cold water if you soaked the dal for over 4 hours, or 5 cups (1.2 liters) of water if you did not soak for that long. Add the turmeric, cinnamon stick, cloves, cardamom pods, and bay leaf/leaves to the pan, and bring to a boil. If any scum rises to the top of the pan once the dal is boiling, remove it with a spoon before putting the dal on to simmer. Cover with a lid, reduce the heat, and simmer the dal for 1–1½ hours. Stir occasionally to make sure it does not stick to the bottom of the pan.

The pan can be taken off the heat when the dal has softened but is not falling apart. Some of the dal may have broken down–leave the remaining lentils unbroken. Add the salt and gently stir to mix it evenly. Set the dal aside for later.

Heat the ghee (or oil) in a skillet over a medium-high heat. If this is your first time frying raisins, make sure to keep a plate and slotted spoon ready to remove them from the pan–this will allow you to do the frying quickly and safely, without scrambling around your kitchen while your raisins overcook and explode! I prefer to take the pan off the heat before I fry them; temperature control is very important to avoid overcooking the delicate raisins. Using a metal spoon, carefully lower the raisins into the hot oil, gently stirring as you do so. The moment they begin to swell and expand, remove the raisins with a slotted spoon and put on a plate. Try to keep as much of the oil in which you fried the raisins in the frying pan.

½ cup (120ml) coconut milk

2 dried red chiles (do not break, as the seeds will escape and make the dal too spicy)

2-in (5-cm) square of fresh or dried (*copra*) coconut, cut into small, flat ¼-in (5-mm) pieces *you can keep the skin on the copra*

2 fresh green chiles, slit lengthways and deseeded, plus extra whole chiles, to garnish *optional*

1 tsp cumin seeds

1½ tsp brown sugar (or 1 heaped tsp white sugar)

Put the pan with the boiled dal back over a medium-low heat, and stir in the coconut milk. Warm through, stirring from time to time to ensure the dal does not get stuck on the base of the pan.

Set the skillet back over a medium heat. When the oil is shimmering, add the dried red chiles. Once the chiles darken, add the coconut pieces and stir-fry for a minute or so, then add the green chiles and cumin seeds. Transfer all the contents of the frying pan to the warm dal, along with the fried raisins and any residual oil that may have come with them. Add the sugar and stir until dissolved. Taste for seasoning and add more salt if required.

If you are not serving the dal immediately, you can cool and refrigerate. When reheating, you may need to add a bit of water to prevent it from drying out.

Serve garnished with whole green chiles, if wished.

*Pictured on pages 200–201*

# Aloo Gobi Bhaji

FRIED POTATOES AND CAULIFLOWER

The essence of this dish is the wholesome, rustic combination of fried potato wedges and cauliflower florets. It truly comes alive when accompanied by sides with some liquid or sauce content, such as raitas and gravy-based dishes. The cauliflower and potatoes can be fried in advance and finished by adding the yogurt right before serving, making them ideal for entertaining guests. They can even make a great side dish at barbecues—a left-field alternative to the traditional potato salad! This recipe can easily be made vegan by substituting the yogurt for a dairy-free alternative.

1lb (450g) white potatoes, peeled and cut into medium-sized wedges
vegetable oil, for deep-frying
2¼lb (1kg) cauliflower, cut into medium florets
3 dried red chiles
1 tsp ground turmeric
½ tsp chili powder
½ tsp freshly ground black pepper
1½ tsp salt
1 tsp roasted cumin powder (see page 29)
1 cup (250g) full-fat yogurt/ crème fraîche/coconut yogurt
chopped herbs (flat-leaf parsley, cilantro, or mint), to garnish

Soak the potato wedges in water for 30 minutes. Rub each wedge to remove any excessive starch on the surface (this makes them easier to fry, as they are less likely to get stuck to the bottom of the pan). Drain and spread on paper towels to dry.

Fill a large, deep saucepan with a 3-in (7.5-cm) depth of vegetable oil and heat over a medium heat. Fry the potato wedges in batches, turning with tongs just until sealed and evenly browned. Do not overcrowd the pan. Remove to drain on paper towels. Once all the potatoes are fried, fry the cauliflower florets in batches just until tinged with brown. You can layer the cauliflower on top of the potato wedges on the paper towels.

Let the oil cool, then strain it into a container. Wipe out the pan with a paper towel.

Add 3 tablespoons of the strained oil back to the pan and heat until shimmering. Add the dried red chiles and stir until they darken, then add the fried potatoes and cauliflower to the pan, followed by the turmeric, chili powder, black pepper, salt, and roasted cumin powder. Continue to stir-fry. To ensure the contents do not get stuck in the pan, use a few tablespoons of water to deglaze the pan. You may need to cover with a lid to steam the contents for a while if they are still uncooked. You want both the potatoes and cauliflower to be cooked through but not falling apart. Once both are cooked, increase the heat and cook off any remaining liquid.

Stir through the yogurt, garnish with chopped herbs, and serve.

You can prepare the potatoes and cauliflower in advance, then reheat, when needed. Add the yogurt and herbs just before serving.

TIP   You can keep the leftover oil to reuse another day, to cook other vegetables or fry eggs.

*Pictured on pages 200–201*

# Saffron & Poppy Seed Kulcha

*Kulcha* are round breads in individual portions from northern India, made by street vendors or in roadside shops. This recipe is an adaptation of the homemade *kulcha* of our family cook Haji Saheb. Made of enriched dough, it has sweet undertones—the perfect accompaniment to a spicy or tangy main dish, such as Jhal Farezi (page 64), but I love having these on their own with a generous pat of salted butter. The base of this bread is *maida*, or white flour. The closest match to Indian *maida* is plain, all-purpose flour, not bread flour. Over time, once you have perfected how to make these, you can try adding other ingredients to replace the poppy seeds, such as herbs, in the dough.

1½ tbsp instant dried yeast

4½ cups (600g) plain flour, plus extra for dusting

1 cup (250ml) melted ghee, coconut oil, or vegetable oil, plus extra for greasing

¼ cup (45g) white sugar

1 tsp salt

warm water, as needed

1½ tbsp milk

good pinch of saffron threads

2 egg yolks, whisked

1 tsp white poppy seeds

In a bowl, add the yeast to the flour and mix well. Add the ghee or coconut/vegetable oil, sugar, and salt, and mix. When the mixture resembles breadcrumbs, add enough warm water to make a firm but pliable dough. Give the dough time to absorb the water before adding more. If you add too much water and the dough gets sticky, add more flour. Transfer to a greased bowl, cover with a damp cloth, and leave to rise in a warm place for about 1 hour, or until doubled in size.

Meanwhile, warm the milk in a saucepan until tepid. Transfer it to a small bowl, add the saffron, and leave it to infuse.

When the dough has doubled in size, remove from the bowl and knock it back on a lightly floured work surface. Divide the dough into 12 equal portions. Cover and leave in a warm place.

Line a baking sheet with a piece of greased parchment paper.

To shape the *kulcha*, roll a portion of the dough into a smooth ball in both hands. Once the ball is smooth, flatten it slightly, and use a rolling pin to roll it out to a circle, 5in (12cm) in diameter. Place it on the baking sheet. Repeat to roll out all the *kulchas*, then cover with a dry cloth and let rise for 30 minutes. I recommend doing this in the oven with the light on, which provides the perfect ambient temperature for the second rise. Remove once risen.

Preheat the oven to 350°F (180°C).

Gently brush the surface of each *kulcha* with the whisked egg yolk and sprinkle with poppy seeds. Bake on the middle shelf of the oven for 15 minutes. Tap the back of a *kulcha*; if it makes a hollow sound, it is done. Drizzle the saffron milk over the *kulchas* and eat warm.

*Pictured on pages 200–201*

# Shorshe Chingri

TIGER PRAWNS WITH MUSTARD

Mustardy seafood dishes are an integral part of Bengali cuisine. This method of "washing" fish or seafood with turmeric and salt is a centuries-old practice that harnesses the antimicrobial properties of turmeric. Even if you have access to the freshest, cleanest seafood, this practice adds a delicate flavor and beautiful color to your seafood, which really complements the mustard in this dish.

1 tbsp black mustard seeds
1 tbsp yellow mustard seeds
splash of distilled malt vinegar
½lb (225g) large raw tiger
   prawns or shrimp, peeled
   and deveined (tails optional)
1 tsp ground turmeric
1 tsp salt, or to taste
2 tbsp neutral oil
2 dried red chiles
1 small onion, grated into a paste
2 garlic cloves, minced
¼-in (5-mm) piece of fresh root
   ginger, peeled and crushed

Soak almost all of the black and yellow mustard seeds in water for 30 minutes, reserving a pinch of each. Drain and add to a pestle and mortar, then add the remaining pinch of each type of mustard seed along with a tiny splash of vinegar, and pound to a grainy consistency.

Wash your prawns or shrimp under cold running water (and devein if this has not already been done for you). Place in a large bowl, add the turmeric and 1 teaspoon salt, and mix gently so the prawns or shrimp are equally coated. Cover and set aside for 5 minutes. Do not refrigerate. The salt will pull moisture out of the seafood; leave this behind in the bowl and discard it.

Heat the oil in a shallow skillet over a medium-high heat, and quickly seal the prawns or shrimp. Remove with a slotted spoon, and place on a plate away from any heat source to minimize residual cooking.

Add the dried red chiles, onion, garlic, and ginger to the pan and fry until aromatic. If the contents stick, add a splash of water to loosen them. Return the prawns or shrimp to the pan and add ½ teaspoon of the grainy mustard from the pestle and mortar. Turn the prawns or shrimp to coat them in the masala and mustard mix, then taste for seasoning. Plate and serve.

# Narangi Pulao

RICE PULAO WITH ORANGES

A common citrusy rice in South India is lemon rice, but rice flavored with oranges is unusual, and this was something I remember being served in my family during the wedding season in the winter. This *pulao* would not be served on the actual day of the wedding–that would always be *biryani*. Instead, this was served in the days building up to the celebration. Once all the clan had descended on the home where the wedding was taking place, there would often be more than a hundred people at every mealtime. This *pulao* goes well with a dish with eggplant or spinach, to balance out the sweet undertones in the rice.

1½ cups (300g) basmati rice
2 large oranges (or 3 smaller oranges)
4 tbsp ghee (or neutral oil, if vegan)
2 whole green cardamom pods
2-in (5-cm) cassia bark (or cinnamon stick)
2 cloves
1 Indian bay leaf
1 medium white onion, halved and thinly sliced into half-moons
2½ cups (600ml) water
1 heaped tsp salt

Wash the rice in a bowl of cold water until the water runs clear. Gently swirling the rice in one direction prevents the delicate tips of the grains from breaking. If the rice is put on to cook with broken tips, they cook faster than the rest of the grains and become glue-like. Careful washing of the rice also makes the dish much healthier as it will have less starch. Once the water is clear, soak the rice for 2 hours in fresh cold water. If you do not have that much time, even 30 minutes of soaking will do.

While the rice is soaking, prepare the oranges. Zest one of the oranges with a vegetable peeler, ensuring you leave the pith behind, and thinly slice the rind into strips. Juice the same orange into a bowl and set aside. Peel and slice the second orange into segments, cover, and set aside in a cool place.

Heat the ghee (or oil) in a large pan over a medium heat, add the cardamom, cassia bark (or cinnamon), cloves, and bay leaf, and stir-fry for a few seconds, then remove the spices from the oil with a slotted spoon to a waiting plate. Try to ensure you leave as much oil in the pan as possible.

Immediately after removing the spices, add the sliced onions to the pan and stir-fry until they turn a caramel brown color. Remove the onions with a slotted spoon, spread them over a plate, and separate them out with a fork so they can cool down and become crisp. Do not spread them on paper towels as they will not become crisp.

In a separate pot, boil the measured water.

Drain the soaked rice and briefly spread it out on paper towels to remove any excess liquid. Do not squeeze the rice as it will break it.

Return the spices and fried onions to the pan set over a medium-high heat, then add the drained rice, followed by the salt, orange rind, and measured boiled water. Cook, uncovered, until almost all the water has been absorbed, then reduce the heat, cover, and cook for a further 5 minutes. Remove the lid, sprinkle the orange juice over the rice, and gently stir with a fork to let any extra moisture evaporate. Garnish with the orange segments before serving.

# Patishapta Pitha

MILK-FILLED PANCAKES

*Patishapta Pitha* is a cherished Bengali dessert–small, crêpe-like pancakes cooked on just one side and rolled around a luscious layer of thickened milk filling. Growing up, my "Ma"–the affectionate name I had for the *ayah* or nanny who raised me–would prepare these delightful treats during school holidays. The kitchen would fill with the sweet aroma of simmering milk and freshly made pancakes, turning ordinary days into treasured memories. While some versions add milk solids (*khoya*) or coconut to deepen the flavor of the filling, a simple filling of sweetened, thickened milk is so simple and moreish.

¾ cup (150g) brown sugar
2 cups (500ml) lukewarm milk, or as needed
1½ cups (250g) rice flour
1¼ cups (150g) plain flour
⅓ cup (50g) semolina
¼ tsp salt
2 tbsp vegetable oil or ghee, for greasing
melted ghee, to serve *optional*

**FOR THE THICKENED MILK FILLING**
12⅔ cups (3 liters) full-fat milk
⅔ cup (130g) brown or white sugar
½ tsp ground cardamom
4 tbsp plain flour
3½oz (100g) *khoya* (milk solids) or ½ cup (30g) grated coconut *optional*

In a large jug, combine the sugar and lukewarm milk, stirring to dissolve. Add the rice flour, plain flour, semolina, and salt. Mix carefully until the batter is smooth and lump-free, with a consistency like pancake batter (adjust the thickness with more milk if needed). Cover the batter and let it rest at room temperature for 3–4 hours. Do not refrigerate.

To make the filling, bring the milk to a gentle boil in a heavy-based pan over a medium-low heat, holding back 4 tablespoons of the milk for later. Stir continuously to prevent the milk from sticking to the base of the pan. Scrape any solids forming on the sides of the pan and incorporate them back into the milk. Gradually stir in the sugar, 1 tablespoon at a time, until it is all dissolved. As the milk reduces and thickens to a creamy consistency, add the ground cardamom. Prepare a paste by mixing the flour into the reserved milk. Stir this paste into the thickened milk and cook for a further 5 minutes. For a more authentic flavor, add the *khoya* (milk solids) or grated coconut and stir well. Remove the pan from the heat and allow the filling to cool.

Grease a nonstick frying pan with a little oil or ghee, and heat over a medium heat. Stir the batter, then use a ladle to spoon about 2 tablespoons of batter into the pan. Spread it evenly with the back of the ladle to form a thin crêpe, about 4–5in (10–12cm) in diameter. Reduce the heat slightly to ensure the crêpe cooks evenly. Cook only on one side until the edges start to release from the pan. Loosen the crêpe from the pan with a spatula and place a strip of the thickened milk filling (about 3in/8cm wide) along one side of the crêpe. Roll up the crêpe and transfer to a plate.

Repeat the process with the remaining batter and filling.

For an extra touch of richness, brush the finished crêpes with melted ghee before serving. Enjoy warm!

# RICE & SPICE

A Meal of Two Halves

*Tehari* is a power-filled rice dish, bursting with flavors of mustard and fresh green chiles. I prefer to eat it as a stand-alone meal with plain yogurt to offset the heat of the green chiles. This rich and satisfying meal is blighted, however, by the absence of vegetables. Splitting your meal into two courses solves the problem. Serving *sardiyon ka shorba*—a warming and hearty spiced vegetable soup—as an appetizer is a great way to introduce the rich and decadent *tehari*. The soup will whet your appetite and the range of vegetables in it provide essential nutrients.

MENU SUGGESTION

**Sardiyon Ka Shorba**
*Sweet*
PAGE 212

**Tehari**
*Spicy*
PAGE 213

# Sardiyon Ka Shorba

A WINTER-WARMER VEGETABLE SOUP

Historically, in the plains of India we do not have a popular soup tradition, while in the colder mountain regions soups are an integral part of the diet. As my father spent most of his childhood and youth in a very British-style boarding school in the Himalayan mountains, he was always happy to have a soup before his meal, even in the heat of the Calcutta summer! This is a carrot and potato soup that is gently spiced—a perfect way to use up the dark-red winter carrots. The carrots can be replaced with any other root vegetable, such as butternut squash or pumpkin.

1¼lb (600g) carrots
⅓lb (150g) potatoes
3 tbsp (50g) salted butter
3 tbsp vegetable oil
1 dried red chile
1-in (2.5-cm) cinnamon stick
1 tsp ground turmeric
1½-in (4-cm) fresh root ginger,
    peeled and roughly chopped
4 garlic cloves, roughly chopped
1 medium onion, finely chopped
½ tsp sugar (any type)
11 cups (2.5 liters) vegetable
    stock
1 tsp salt, or to taste

**IF MAKING YOUR OWN STOCK
(OPTIONAL)**

13 cups (3 liters) water
1 medium onion, halved (skin on)
1 bay leaf
1 tbsp black peppercorns
good pinch of salt

If making your own stock (a good non-waste option), peel the carrots and potatoes, and add the peels to a large pan with the measured water. Bring to a boil, then add the onion, bay leaf, and peppercorns, and a good pinch of salt. Cover and simmer for 1 hour.

Strain the stock through a fine-mesh strainer or doubled cheesecloth before use.

Cut the carrots and potatoes into 1-in (2.5-cm) cubes. Start preparing the soup once the stock is strained and ready.

Heat the butter and oil in a large saucepan over a medium heat. Add the dried red chile and give it a few seconds to darken and release its smoky aroma. Add the cinnamon stick, turmeric, ginger, garlic, chopped onion, sugar, carrots, and potatoes. Stir to coat the vegetables with the oil and butter. Add the stock and bring to a boil. You do not need to cover the soup. Reduce the heat and simmer for 30 minutes, or until the potatoes and carrots are fork tender. Remove from the heat and let cool slightly. Add salt, to taste.

Remove the cinnamon stick and dried red chile from the soup, then blend it to a smooth, creamy texture. Taste and adjust the seasoning, if required. Serve in warmed bowls to retain the heat of the soup.

*Pictured on page 210*

# Tehari

## SPICY BEEF PULAO

From *pulao* and *pilaf* to *biryani,* hearty rice and meat dishes are mainstays of the cuisines of the subcontinent and neighboring countries. These aren't recipes that were taught in cookbooks but passed down through generations of matriarchs and spread along the Silk Road by horseback. Pungent mustard oil and fiery, fresh green chiles make *Tehari* a robust and bold dish best eaten with a side of plain yogurt or salad. I always ask my family to make this dish for me when I visit them in Dhaka. They make *Tehari* with the small-grained Kalijeera rice, which has the most beautiful aroma. The tiny grains absorb the beef broth, adding an unmatched depth and intensity of flavor. As the small-grain rice is not easily available outside the region, I usually cook this with basmati rice, which works well.

2¼lb (1kg) beef, cut into 1½-in (4-cm) cubes
½ cup (125g) plain yogurt
2 tsp salt
1 tbsp ginger paste
1 tbsp garlic paste
1 tsp ground coriander
1 tsp cumin seeds
½ tsp ground turmeric
½ tsp chili powder
¾ cup (180ml) mustard oil
¼ cup (80g) thinly sliced onions
3 green cardamom pods
2 bay leaves
3 cloves
2-in (5-cm) cassia bark (or cinnamon stick)
6 cups (1.5 liters) water
2½ cups (500g) Kalijeera or basmati rice
5–6 green chiles

Place the meat in a large bowl and marinate with the yogurt, ½ teaspoon of the salt, ginger and garlic pastes, ground coriander, cumin seeds, turmeric, and chili powder for 2 hours.

Heat ¼ cup (60ml) of the oil, in a deep, heavy-based pan that has a lid, over a medium heat. Add half of the sliced onions and fry until brown. Remove with a slotted spoon to a plate.

To the same pan, add the cardamom pods, bay leaves, and cloves, then add the marinated meat and cook, stirring, for 25–30 minutes. Add the cassia bark and cook for a minute or two until it is dried out and slightly toasted, then add the fried onions along with 2 cups (500ml) of the water. Bring to a boil, cover, and reduce to a low simmer for 1½ hours.

When the meat is ready, in a separate heavy-based pan with a lid, heat the remaining ½ cup (125ml) of oil over a medium heat, and fry the remaining sliced onions until brown. Remove with a slotted spoon and reserve, then add the uncooked rice to the pan and toast for 5 minutes.

Meanwhile, bring the remaining 4 cups (1 liter) of water to a boil. Add the remaining ¾ teaspoon of salt.

When the rice has toasted, add the boiling water to the pan and bring back to a boil, then add the meat mixture. Cover, reduce the heat, and simmer for 30 minutes.

Remove the lid from the pan, stir, and add the green chiles, then cover again and place the pan on a *tawa* or cast-iron skillet (over the same low heat), and leave undisturbed for 1 hour. After this time it is ready to serve, garnished with the reserved fried onions.

*Pictured on page 210*

– Rice & spice –

# Saunf Elaichi Chai

FENNEL SEED AND CARDAMOM-SPICED CHAI

As mothers of a certain generation in India will tell you—*saunf* (or fennel seeds), boiled, cooled, and filtered in water was an effective natural remedy for a baby with gripe or colic. Over time, this practice for children fell out of use, but it remained a tradition for adults as an effective spice to help indigestion, either eaten raw or boiled in water and made into a tea. This is a healing and restorative tea, which helps gut health but also is great to drink at the end of the day.

2 green cardamom pods
1 tbsp fennel seeds
1½ cups (350ml) water
3 tbsp Assam or Kenyan tea
    leaves (or 3–4 teabags)
1 cup (240ml) full-fat milk
3 tbsp sugar (any type)

Begin by opening your cardamom seeds with the side of your knife and (optionally) crushing the fennel seeds in a pestle and mortar. Crushing and opening your spices helps them impart more intense flavors to your tea. Leaving them whole will produce a more subtly flavored tea.

Bring the measured water to a boil in a saucepan, then add the tea leaves (or bags) and spices. Once this is at a rolling boil, reduce the heat to medium-low and boil for at least 2 minutes, longer if you want a strong cup of tea. Some black teas, like Assam, can become very astringent if steeped for too long, so be sure to taste periodically if you want to steep your tea for much longer. If you are using teabags, make sure to remove them after 2 minutes. Steeping teabags for too long can leave behind an unpleasant, papery flavor profile. You can add fresh teabags to your pan at any point if your tea is not strong enough.

Add the milk and sugar, return the tea to a rolling boil, and simmer again over a medium-low heat for at least another 2 minutes.

Turn off the heat and, using a ladle, aerate the tea a few times by pulling a ladleful of tea out and pouring it back into the pan from as high as you can safely manage. Strain your *chai* and serve in cups.

বসন্ত

◇ 6 ◇

# BÔSHONTO

Spring

Spring is the season of rebirth, renewal, and regeneration. After months of lying dormant beneath the earth, seeds finally break free, sprouting into new life as the world around us awakens. It's a time of fresh beginnings, where the warmth in the air invites us to step outside, reconnect, and share meals with those we love. Spring offers the perfect opportunity to break bread and form new connections, especially as the longer, lighter evenings encourage gatherings with friends and family.

One recipe that shines in any season, but especially in spring, is Lutchi (page 246). These soft, golden, puffy breads are a staple in my kitchen—both at my restaurant in London and every time I'm fortunate enough to return home. Lutchis are a true crowd-pleaser and a versatile addition to your cooking repertoire. Whether served at a family dinner or a festive gathering, they always bring people together, making them the perfect companion to the spirit of spring.

# SPRING LUNCH

## A Meal for One

The combination of an orange-based salad with a peanut chutney on the side provides a good mix of vitamins from the oranges and fiber from the peanuts. With so many contrasting flavors, the more simply flavored fish pakora is a good source of protein. It also takes very little time to cook. This is the perfect meal to prepare if you are cooking just for yourself, as you can prepare only as much salad and fish as you need, minimizing food waste. Even if you are working from home, this lunch can be prepared in a short time with very little mess. The cleanup after preparing a meal is often a psychological deterrent for someone cooking just for themselves, but this menu requires minimal cookware and bowls. The peanut chutney can be added to a meal the next day, and can even be eaten with something like pasta, baked potato, or grilled chicken from your favorite takeout. This is worth its weight in time investment for midweek, midday nourishment.

### MENU SUGGESTION

**Fish Pakora**
*Sour & Spicy*
PAGE 222

**Narangi Salad**
*Spicy*
PAGE 224

**Moongaphalee Chutney**
*Salty*
PAGE 225

# Fish Pakora

These versatile fried fish fritters can be served as a starter, as a canapé, or as part of a meal. The combination of gram flour (*besan*) and rice flour gives the batter a nice texture, and the layering of flavors in this pakora all comes together when fried. If your early attempts at making this pakora do not turn out as you had hoped, please persist and try again. Adjusting the oil temperature when frying, or the thickness of the batter in which the fish is fried, as well as ensuring the fish is completely dry when it is battered, all make a huge difference to the finished product. Once you perfect this recipe, it will become part of your repertoire! Serve with a chutney, such as the cilantro chutney on page 25 or peanut chutney on page 225.

2⅔lb (1.2kg) firm, white fish fillets (cod, barramundi, bhekti)
1 tsp ground turmeric
3 tbsp lime juice
1½ tbsp ginger paste
1 tsp garlic paste
1 tbsp ground coriander
1 tsp ground cumin
1½ tsp salt
¾ cup (90g) gram flour (*besan*)
5 tbsp rice flour
1 tsp chili powder
vegetable oil, for deep-frying

Cut the fish into thick pieces—try to cut all the pieces to a similar size. The width of the pieces will depend on the fish you are using. Ideally, each piece should be 5–6in (12–15cm) long. Pat these dry with a paper towel and gently massage with the turmeric.

In a bowl, combine the lime juice, ginger and garlic pastes, ground coriander, cumin, and salt. Add the fish pieces and coat well. Set aside to marinate for 15 minutes. Discard any water that may come out of the fish.

In a shallow bowl, combine both flours with the chili powder and add water, a little at a time, whisking until you have a thick, smooth batter. The desired consistency is one that "drops" and does not pour from a spoon.

Heat enough oil for deep-frying in a *karai* or wok over a medium-high heat. Completely coat one fish fillet in the batter, then add to the hot oil and fry for 3–4 minutes. Remove with a slotted spoon to drain on a paper towel. When cool enough to touch, taste the fish for seasoning and adjust the lime/salt/chili to your preference, bearing in mind the chutney you will serve alongside.

Finish frying all the fish in the same way as the trial piece. Do not overcrowd the pan—fry 3–4 pieces at a time.

Eat while still hot, with a chutney for dipping.

TIP   If you are making these for a party, it may be easier to use a deep-fat fryer with a lid to make these just before serving.

# Narangi Salad

SPICED ORANGE SALAD

For a hot, sultry country, India does not have a huge range of salads compared to Mediterranean or Levantine cuisines. This does not mean we do not eat fresh vegetables with our meals—it is usual for a family to have slices of onion, tomatoes, radish, and cucumber on a plate. Sometimes these vegetables are served sprinkled with salt, pepper, and chaat masala or dried mango powder (*amchur*), with thick wedges of lime for squeezing over. This salad is similar to the idea of combining a mix of vegetables with a zingy, citrusy dressing. It goes well with heavy, spicy meats in gravy.

1 tbsp cider vinegar

3 fresh green or red chiles, deseeded and thinly sliced

4 garlic cloves, finely chopped

1¾–2lb (800–900g) large oranges

⅓lb (150g) carrots, thinly sliced

½lb (225g) red cabbage, thinly sliced

1 tbsp honey

1 tbsp lemon juice

1 tsp salt

½ tsp freshly ground black pepper

1 tsp vegetable oil

¼ tsp nigella seeds

4 tbsp chopped fresh cilantro leaves, to garnish

¼ tsp chili (red pepper) flakes *optional*

Place the vinegar in a bowl and add the chiles and garlic. Set aside to infuse.

Cut the oranges to remove the skin and the white pith, then remove the segments. Do this over a plate so you can save any juice that comes out and add that to the salad. Place the segments and any juices in a bowl. Add the sliced carrots and red cabbage.

To the vinegar mixture, add the honey, lemon juice, salt, and pepper, and whisk with a fork. Pour the dressing over the orange salad and mix well. Taste for seasoning.

Heat the vegetable oil in a small pan, then add the nigella seeds. Pour over the salad and stir with a spoon, to evenly distribute it through the salad. Garnish with chopped fresh cilantro before serving.

The chili flakes are optional. If you are serving this salad at a party, you could serve them on the side in a bowl, and anyone wanting to add more chili to the salad can do so.

*Pictured on page 223*

# Moongaphalee Chutney

PEANUT CHUTNEY

This is a spicy, aromatic chutney that goes with almost anything. I have eaten this chutney with poached eggs, baked potato, goat's cheese, and with sourdough and butter! The role of a chutney or pickle in a meal is not given the importance it deserves. These are the additions that often bring the zing, heat, and tang to a meal. The addition of a pickle or chutney with plain rice or roti/paratha transforms a meal from simple to complex flavors. I have not tried different alternatives to peanut, but I am sure cashews or almonds would work as well—maybe even pine nuts.

4 tbsp grated fresh coconut (or desiccated/dried shredded coconut)

½lb (225g) raw unroasted peanuts (with skin or skinless)

1 tsp cumin seeds

½ tsp fenugreek seeds

1 tbsp vegetable oil

2 dried red chiles

1 tsp *urad dal*

10 fresh curry leaves (optional, do not use dried)

1 tsp brown sugar

2 tsp salt

2 tbsp lime juice

If you are using desiccated coconut, add some warm (not boiling water) to a bowl and mix the coconut in. The texture should resemble well-cooked oatmeal. Do not drown the coconut, as it will slowly absorb the water and become softer. Mix the water all the way through the coconut, and let soak while you roast the peanuts.

Dry-roast the peanuts in a heavy-based pan, over a medium heat for 12–15 minutes, until well roasted. Stir constantly with a wooden spoon to ensure that the peanuts are evenly roasted. If any peanuts burn, discard them. If the peanuts are skinless, you will see them glistening as you roast them. Transfer them to a plate and spread them out to cool. If the peanuts have skins on them, rub away the skins. Wipe the pan with a paper towel to remove any residual oil from the peanuts.

In the same pan, dry-roast the cumin seeds and fenugreek seeds over a medium heat. Once the seeds have darkened, transfer them to a bowl.

Add the oil to the pan, then add the dried red chiles, *urad dal*, and curry leaves (if using), and stir-fry very briefly, until fragrant. The *urad dal* just needs to begin to change color. Transfer to the same bowl as the roasted seeds to cool.

When cool, remove the stalk of the dried red chiles (if any), and break into pieces. Tear the curry leaves into smaller pieces. Transfer all the contents of the bowl to a grinder or food processor. Add the soaked desiccated or fresh coconut, sugar, salt, lime juice, and finally the peanuts, then grind to a rough paste. This chutney will last for a week in the fridge.

*Pictured on page 223*

# Stuffed Bitter Gourd

Bitter gourd is an acquired taste. It's a much-loved vegetable of Bengal and is often eaten at the start of a meal to stimulate the palate. This recipe is one of the ways in which I enjoy this bitter vegetable. The salting and boiling effectively reduce the bitterness. The stuffing has gentle spicing, and the combination of coconut and almonds are a good balance for the bitter flavor of the vegetable. You can swap the almonds for cashews, or any nuts you have in the house, but avoid walnuts, as you want to balance the bitter flavors in this dish, not add to them! If you cannot find any coconut, use a combination of almonds and finely chopped dried apricots or any dried fruit. Do not use any substitute that is moist, as it will make the stuffing too wet.

6 small bitter gourds, washed and dried *select lighter-colored gourds, ideally 3–4in (7.5–10cm) in length; if they are longer, use just 4*

2 heaped tsp salt

2½ cups (600ml) water

1 tsp coriander seeds

½ tsp cumin seeds

¼ tsp fennel seeds

1½ tsp brown sugar

½ cup (50g) blanched almonds (skinless)

3 tbsp grated fresh coconut *do not use desiccated (dried shredded); frozen coconut is an option if you cannot find fresh, brought to room temperature*

½ tsp ground turmeric

¼ tsp chili powder

1–2 tbsp warm water

6 tbsp vegetable oil

Make a clean slit in the middle of each gourd with a sharp knife. Ensure the slit is not all the way from top to bottom, as it will be harder to seal and fry after stuffing. Use a small spoon to scoop out and discard all the pulp and seeds. (The seeds are relished in Bengal—you can roast them and add them to salads if you enjoy the flavor.) Rub 1½ teaspoons of salt on the insides and outsides of the gourds, and set aside for 30–40 minutes. After this time, gently squeeze the gourds to get rid of any excess liquid.

Bring the measured water to a rolling boil in a deep saucepan, add the gourds, and boil for 5 minutes. If you are using larger gourds, they may need a couple more minutes. Remove the gourds to a bowl of cold water to stop the cooking process. Leave in the cold water for 5 minutes, then remove and gently pat dry with paper towels. Dry the insides too, being careful not to tear the slits when dabbing.

Dry-roast the coriander, cumin, and fennel seeds in a heavy-based pan over a low heat, stirring frequently. Do not roast spices on thin-based pans, as they may not diffuse heat evenly and the spices may burn quickly. Slow-roasting whole seeds and spices elevates their flavors, as the heat permeates all the way through and the smoky/roasted aromas are heightened. Transfer to a plate and leave to cool.

Pulse the cooled seeds to a powder in a spice grinder along with the brown sugar, blanched nuts, coconut, and remaining ½ teaspoon of salt. Transfer to a bowl and add the turmeric and chili powder. Add the warm water in drips to make a stuffing that holds together. Do not make it wet, or it will leak out of the gourd when you stuff it. It should have the texture of peanut butter. Stuff the gourds with the mixture, using a table knife to push it into the slits. Seal and tie with string or sewing thread (thick cooking twine will damage the gourds).

Heat the oil in a large, deep, heavy-based frying pan over a medium-high heat. Add the gourds in a single layer. When they start to sizzle, reduce the heat to medium and cook for about 20 minutes, turning periodically to ensure all the sides of the gourd are cooked. When the outsides are crisp and tinged with brown, remove from the pan, cut the string, and serve immediately, ideally with rice.

# A DINNER
# FOR RENEWAL

Vegetarian

The arrival of spring is a much-needed reminder of the power of nature. In the ashes of winter, we see the embers of life and rebirth. Eating well is our way to give our bodies a boost and build our resilience. Iron-rich spinach, fortified with turmeric-rich *qubooli* (rice and lentil *pulao*), provides a vitamin boost in a meal that empowers and strengthens. Pineapple *pachadi* has sour flavors that complement and intensify the tangy notes of yogurt in the *qubooli*. This is a great pick-me-up meal.

MENU SUGGESTION

**Qubooli**
*Sweet*
PAGE 230

**Saag Aloo**
*Bitter*
PAGE 234

**Pineapple Pachadi**
*Sweet & Sour*
PAGE 235

# Qubooli

HYDERABADI TANGY RICE AND LENTIL PULAO

This *pulao* is a more complex version of *kichadi*, a distinctive, tangy, Hyderabadi dish of rice and lentils cooked together with yogurt. The dal and rice are cooked separately and are then combined with spices to make a dish that is a complete meal on its own.

**QUBOOLI GARAM MASALA**
8 cloves
4 large black cardamom pods
1 tsp black peppercorns
2 cassia bark sticks

**FOR THE DAL**
¾ cup (150g) *channa dal*
2 cups (500ml) water
¼ tsp ground turmeric

**FOR THE RICE**
2 cups (400g) basmati rice
8½ cups (2 liters) water
1 tbsp salt

For the *Qubooli* garam masala, heat a heavy-based, dry frying pan over a medium heat. Dry-roast the whole spices until aromatic, then transfer to a plate to cool. When cool, grind to a fine powder. Store in an airtight container.

Wash the *channa dal* and soak in a large bowl of fresh water for 3 hours.

After an hour, wash the rice in a bowl of cold water, gently swirling in one direction only, until the water runs clear. This prevents the delicate tips of the rice grains from breaking. The broken tips are not visible and will stay in the pan with the rest of the rice. Those tiny tips will cook much faster because of their size and become like glue as you continue to cook the rice. This will ruin a dish like *Qubooli*. Careful washing of the rice ensures you achieve the fluffy texture you want, and makes the dish much healthier as it will have less starch. When the water runs clear, drain and place in a bowl of fresh water to soak for 2 hours.

Drain the soaked rice and spread on a paper towel to dry. Boil the rice in the measured water with the salt, until three-quarters cooked. To check this, take out one grain of rice from the water and crush between your thumb and two fingers. When most of the grain becomes mush but there is still a hard core left in the center, this is the time to drain the rice. Spread out the partially cooked rice on a tray to cool.

Drain the dal, then boil it in the measured water with the turmeric for 20–25 minutes. Do not cover or add any salt, and do not stir too much as you need the dal to remain whole. Drain and spread over a tray to cool.

**TO BUILD THE PULAO**

6 tbsp vegetable oil
½ cup (150g) brown onions,
    thinly sliced into half-moons
1 tbsp ginger paste
1 tsp garlic paste
⅔ cup (150g) plain yogurt
4 tbsp ghee
3 green chiles, chopped
2 tbsp chopped fresh
    cilantro leaves
1½ tbsp chopped fresh
    mint leaves
6½ tbsp (100ml) warm milk
¼ tsp saffron strands, soaked
    in 1 tbsp tepid milk
2 tbsp lemon juice
salt, to taste

**EQUIPMENT**

large heavy-based pot with a lid,
    at least 6in (15cm) deep and
    8in (20cm) in diameter

Heat the oil in a frying pan over a medium heat, and fry the onions until caramelized and crisp. Remove with a slotted spoon, and spread on a plate with a fork to ensure the onions cool quickly.

To the same oil, add the ginger and garlic pastes, and stir for a few minutes (add sprays of water if anything gets stuck). Once the garlic has lost its raw smell, start adding the yogurt, 1 tablespoon at a time, until each addition looks dried and crumbly. Transfer the entire contents of the pan to a bowl and set aside.

In your large, heavy-based pot, start layering the *pulao*. Grease the inside of the pot with 2 tablespoons of the ghee. Add one-third of the rice and spread in a layer. Drizzle some of the garlic-ginger-yogurt-oil on top of the rice. Add half of the dal in a layer, then add half of the chopped chiles, cilantro, and mint on top. Layer one-third of the rice on top again. Crumble half of the crispy onions on top of the rice, then add the remaining dal, and pour over the warm milk and the remaining garlic-ginger-yogurt-oil. Add the remaining green chiles, cilantro, and mint, then add the final layer of rice. Drizzle with the remaining 2 tablespoons of ghee, the saffron-infused milk, and remaining crispy onions, then top with all the *Qubooli* garam masala. Set the pot, uncovered, over a medium-high heat and wait until it is steaming. Put an iron skillet or *tawa* under the pot and keep the heat on medium for a further 2–3 minutes. Place a clean kitchen cloth on top of the pot and put the lid on, then reduce the heat and leave for 15 minutes.

After 15 minutes, remove the lid, add the lemon juice, and gently mix the rice. Check the seasoning, adding salt if needed. Turn the heat off, but leave the pot on the skillet, covered, to rest for 30 minutes. Eat with a crunchy vegetable or salad.

*Pictured on pages 232–233*

# Saag Aloo

POTATOES AND SPINACH

This dish, although traditionally made with spinach, can be made with any greens, such as kale or mustard greens. Over winter, we would have this dish very often at home in India, as the spinach season was short, and my mother would always remind us about the strengthening power of spinach and Popeye the Sailor! My children would probably roll their eyes if I tried that tactic on them today. This recipe can be made with frozen spinach, too.

4 tbsp vegetable oil
1 tsp cumin seeds
1 large onion, finely chopped
1 tbsp ginger paste
1 tsp garlic paste
1 tbsp ground coriander
1 tsp ground turmeric
1 tsp Kashmiri red chili powder
1 large tomato, finely chopped
1lb (450g) white potatoes,
   peeled and chopped
   into small cubes
2 tsp salt
½ cup (125ml) water
32oz (1kg) fresh spinach leaves

Heat the oil, in a deep saucepan with a lid, over a medium heat until shimmering. Add the cumin seeds followed by the chopped onion. Stir until the onions take on a brown tinge and the cumin seeds are fragrant. Add the ginger and garlic pastes, stir for a minute, or until fragrant, then add the ground coriander, turmeric, and chili powder, and stir until the spices begin releasing their beautiful aromas. Add the tomato and potatoes, followed by the salt. Add the measured water, bring to the boil, then cover and simmer for 5 minutes.

Remove the lid and continue cooking until the potatoes are fork tender. Add the spinach and stir until it wilts and the liquid released has evaporated. Taste and adjust the seasoning, then serve.

*Pictured on pages 232–233*

# Pineapple Pachadi

YOGURT WITH PINEAPPLE

I lived in South India for eight years and I remember this pineapple dish from my childhood in Madras (now Chennai). This is also a recipe made in Kerala. The layering of flavors in this dish makes this the perfect accompaniment to a barbecue, as the combination of sweet and sour from the pineapple and yogurt is a great foil for rich roasted or grilled meats. The *pachadi* is served at room temperature and is a great dish for entertaining, as it can be made in advance and transferred to the serving dish, then served when required. If mustard oil is not available, use 2 teaspoons of vegetable oil and skip the smoking step.

½lb (225g) fresh pineapple, cut into ½-in (1-cm) cubes
½ cup (120ml) water
1 tsp salt
1 cup (240g) fresh coconut powder
1 cup (250g) plain yogurt, whisked
1 tsp mustard oil
2 tsp vegetable oil
1 tsp mustard seeds
6 shallots, thinly sliced
3 dried red chiles, broken
½ tsp ground turmeric
6 curry leaves

In a saucepan, combine the pineapple, measured water, and salt, and boil until all the water has evaporated or has been absorbed, and the pineapple pieces have softened. Add the coconut powder and cook for a further 2 minutes. Remove from the heat and let cool, then add the yogurt.

In a separate pan, heat the mustard oil until it is smoking hot (to reduce its pungency), then add the vegetable oil and bring it back to a medium heat. Add the mustard seeds, shallots, dried chiles, turmeric, and curry leaves, stir, and cook until the shallots are tinged with brown on the edges. Pour the contents of the pan over the pineapple and yogurt mixture.

*Pictured on pages 232–233*

# Shikanji

### A GINGER AND LIME DRINK

*Shikanji* is a distinctive, lightly salted and spiced lemonade that is enjoyed across the Indian subcontinent. This is a ginger and lime variation. The salt and spices in this drink give it hydrating and cooling properties that are lifesavers in the intense Indian heat. Unlike my Aam Panna recipe (page 82), this does not produce a concentrate, so is therefore simpler and easier to prepare on the day. This makes it great for entertaining at short notice. In India, lemons are traditionally used to make *shikanji*, but the lemons in India are smaller and closer to the limes available in the West in flavor. This has informed my decision to recommend limes, but feel free to use any other citrus of your choice to make a unique variation of this *shikanji*.

2-in (5-cm) piece of fresh root
    ginger, peeled
12 limes
8 tbsp white sugar
1 tbsp Himalayan pink salt
1 tbsp crushed black pepper
1 tbsp roasted cumin powder
    (page 25)
1 tsp dried mango
    powder (*amchur*)
6¾ cups (1.5 liters) chilled water
handful of ice cubes, plus extra
    to serve
fresh mint sprigs and
    lemon wedges, to garnish

Grate the ginger with a microplane grater or zester over some cheesecloth. Squeeze the juice out over a bowl and reserve the shredded ginger to be used as ginger paste in another recipe.

Squeeze the juice of the limes into a separate bowl.

Add the lime juice, 1–2 tablespoons of the ginger juice, the sugar, spices, chilled water, and a handful of ice cubes to a blender, and blend until smooth.

Serve in tall glasses over ice, garnished with fresh mint sprigs and a lemon wedge.

*Pictured on page 238*

# Thandai

### FENNEL-INFUSED SWEET MILK DRINK

*Thandai* is made by steeping a paste of nuts and spices in milk to produce a refreshing, cooling drink for the fervent activity and spring heat of Holi. This nutty, delicately spiced drink is a central part of the festivities every year. *Thandai* can be enjoyed hot or cold, but is traditionally served over ice in terra-cotta cups.

½ cup (50g) almonds
⅓ cup (45g) pistachios
⅓ cup (45g) cashew nuts
12 black peppercorns
2 tbsp watermelon seeds
2 tbsp poppy seeds
1½ tbsp fennel seeds
4 tbsp dried rose petals
1 cup (250ml) room-
    temperature water
seeds from 10 green
    cardamom pods
½ cup (120g) white sugar
    (or *sharakara*)
generous pinch of saffron
    threads

**TO SERVE**
1 cup (250ml) chilled
    full-fat milk
dried rose petals, to garnish

Soak the nuts, peppercorns, seeds, and rose petals in the measured water overnight. If you are pressed for time, you can soak this mixture for 1–2 hours in warm water.

Pour the entire contents of the bowl into a blender along with the cardamom, sugar, and saffron. Blend until you have a smooth paste. Regular white sugar will work perfectly well here, but if you can, use *sharakara*. This form of sugar is made of unrefined sugar cane, and is much more flavorful.

To serve, add 4 tablespoons of the *thandai* paste to a glass or cocktail shaker and add the milk. Mix or shake thoroughly until combined. Strain and serve over ice, garnished with rose petals.

You can also make this drink in a large jug or pitcher, using the ratio of 4 tablespoons of paste to 1 cup of milk. This will keep in the fridge for up to 2 days. If you have terra-cotta cups, *thandai* is best enjoyed out of these. Keeping your *thandai*, chilled, in these cups will impart a gorgeous petrichor note to your *thandai*, which I really love.

*Pictured on page 238*

# FESTIVE FEAST

A Kaleidoscope of Flavors

From Easter to Persian Nowruz, Japanese cherry blossom festivals or Holi, the festival of colors in India, springtime is marked the world over with festivities and food. If you are celebrating a spring festival with friends and family, this is the perfect combination of dishes to serve. The chicken *kabab* is called *hariyali*, which means "greenery." This word is not just used literally to describe foliage, it is often used by adults to younger members of the family to wish that their homes are filled with abundance and that they thrive. Greenery is always a sign of life and hope! In this meal, the fish with peppers and the apricot chutney bring different textures and flavors of sweetness and tanginess. *Lutchis* are a good bread to serve, but any store-bought bread would also work, as the idea of making bread for a large gathering is too daunting.

MENU SUGGESTION

**Hariyali Chicken Kabab**
*Salty*
PAGE 242

**Shimla Mirch Machli**
*Sweet*
PAGE 243

**Lutchi**
*Sweet*
**page 246**

**Khoobani Chutney**
*Pungent*
PAGE 247

# Hariyali Chicken Kabab

These chicken skewers make a great addition to your barbecue repertoire. The addition of yogurt acts like a shield that prevents the chicken from burning. Of course, it is still possible to dry this *kabab* out by overcooking it! If you are making this for the family, or adults who do not like chiles, you can eliminate the green chiles and add a bit of black pepper to the marinade instead. This goes well with the Narangi Salad (page 224).

1¼ cups (20g) fresh mint leaves, roughly chopped

1¼ cups (20g) fresh cilantro leaves, roughly chopped

3 garlic cloves, roughly chopped

2½-in (6-cm) fresh root ginger, peeled and roughly chopped

3 tbsp lemon juice

½ cup (100g) plain yogurt

1 tsp ground turmeric

1 tbsp ground coriander

1 tsp sugar (any type)

2 tsp salt

2 tsp chili powder

1½lb (750g) skinless and boneless chicken thighs, cut into 1-in (2.5-cm) cubes

2 tbsp melted butter, for basting

4 green chiles, to garnish

1 tsp toasted sesame seeds, to garnish

**EQUIPMENT**

6 metal skewers (for barbecuing) or bamboo skewers (for broiling)

Combine the fresh mint and cilantro in a blender with the garlic and ginger, and pulse until smooth. You may need to add a little water to get the desired consistency. Transfer to a large bowl, add the lemon juice, yogurt, turmeric, ground coriander, sugar, salt, and chili powder, and mix well. Add the chicken pieces and mix thoroughly. Cover and leave to marinate in the fridge for a minimum of 2 hours, or ideally overnight.

Bring the chicken to room temperature before cooking.

If you are cooking on an outdoor barbecue, divide the chicken among 6 metal skewers. If you are cooking in the oven on a broiler and are using bamboo skewers, soak the skewers in cold water for 30 minutes to ensure they do not burn. Cook over a medium-low heat for about 5 minutes on each side, basting with the melted butter, and turning the skewers at regular intervals to ensure even cooking. If broiling, keep the *kababs* 4–5in (10–12cm) away from the heat.

*Pictured on pages 244–245*

# Shimla Mirch Machli

FISH IN RED PEPPER AND COCONUT GRAVY

This fish would be made in my home when there was a glut of peppers in the bazaar and the price had fallen. It was not unusual for vegetable vendors in the market to add a couple of bunches of cilantro leaves and some green chiles, free, to every customer. I watched this for years as a child when I would accompany my mother to the bazaar. During peak pepper season, the vegetable vendor was always keen to get my mother to buy his entire stock. His powers of persuasion were impressive, from telling her that the vitamins would be good for the children, he would then switch to emotional blackmail telling her that the peppers would fetch a lower price tomorrow as they would no longer look so fresh, then offering her an "unmissable" discount. My mother almost always took the bait—we would come home with 11 pounds (5 kilograms) of extra peppers and then find them used in a variety of our dishes.

½ tsp ground turmeric

1 tsp chili powder

1½ tsp salt

2¼lb (1kg) firm white fish
   (fillet, loin, or thick steaks),
   cut into roughly 6 portions

½ cup (125ml) vegetable oil

1 tsp mustard seeds

2 bay leaves

2 dried red chiles

¾ cup (200g) Spanish or white
   onions, thinly sliced into
   half-moons

2-in (5-cm) fresh root ginger,
   thinly sliced

6 garlic cloves, thinly sliced

2 large red bell peppers, cut
   into 1-in (2.5-cm) cubes

good pinch of sugar (any type)

8–10 cherry or small tomatoes
   *optional*

2 x 13.5fl oz cans (800ml) of
   coconut milk

2½–3 tbsp lemon juice *optional*

chopped fresh cilantro,
   to garnish

Mix together ¼ teaspoon of the turmeric, ½ teaspoon of the chili powder, and ¾ teaspoon of the salt, and rub on the fish portions. Set aside on a plate for 30 minutes. Discard any liquid that comes out of the fish.

Heat half of the oil in a frying pan over a medium heat. Add the mustard seeds and wait for them to pop before adding the bay leaves. Stir for a few seconds, then add the dried red chiles and the onions, and stir until they start to brown. Add the ginger and garlic, and continue to stir for a moment. Add the red pepper cubes and continue to fry. When the edges of the peppers are tinged with brown and curling, transfer the contents of the pan to a plate to cool.

Use a paper towel to wipe the pan clean, add the remaining oil, and warm over a medium heat. Gently squeeze the marinated fish pieces to remove excess moisture. Place two pieces at a time in the hot oil, and cook to seal the fish on both sides. Do not let the fish cook all the way through, it should just brown on the outside. Fry all the pieces and transfer to a tray. Let the remaining oil sit in the pan—this oil will form the base of the gravy.

Discarding the bay leaves, transfer the cooled, red-pepper mixture to a blender and whizz to a smooth paste.

Reheat the oil in which the fish was fried and add the red-pepper paste. Keep stirring until the oil comes to the edges of the pan, then add the remaining turmeric, chili powder, and salt, along with the sugar, and continue to stir (add the cherry tomatoes at this stage if you are using them). Transfer the fish pieces back to the pan and add three-quarters of the coconut milk. Reduce the heat and simmer for 10–15 minutes, until the fish is cooked. Add lemon juice (if using), then taste for seasoning and adjust.

Before serving, pour the remaining coconut milk over the fish, and garnish with chopped cilantro.

*Pictured on pages 244–245*

# Lutchi

BENGALI-STYLE PUFFED BREAD

This is a quintessential Bengali fried puffed bread, which is made with *maida* or white flour. Historically, the flour in India was low in gluten, as the wheat was a softer variety than the harder wheat grown in colder climates, which had to withstand harsher winters. The soft, puffy breads are the most glorious accompaniment to dishes like Aloo Dum (page 135) and Choler Dal (page 198). Usually, *lutchis* are small, just 3–4 bites each. Puffy *lutchis* are very difficult to perfect, and require holding the oil at a steady, carefully controlled temperature. They require evenly, thinly rolled dough, and close attention when cooking to ensure they puff up without burning. It can take a few tries to master the technique—don't be discouraged if things don't immediately work out.

1¾ cups (250g) *maida* flour
(or plain flour)
½ tsp salt
¼ tsp white sugar
2 tbsp melted ghee
½–⅔ cup (120–150ml) warm
water
vegetable oil, for greasing and
deep-frying

Sift the flour into a bowl, add the salt and sugar, and mix. Add the ghee and mix thoroughly with your hands until the texture resembles oats. Make a well in the middle, and add the warm water slowly. Knead with your knuckles and start to gather the flour together in one ball. Adding water in stages is better, as you will not end up with a soggy dough. In case you do, just add more flour and continue to knead. Once the dough has a smooth texture, cover with a damp cloth and set aside for at least 45 minutes. The dough does not have to rise, so it does not have to be left in a warm place.

Divide the dough into 12 portions and roll each one into a tight, seamless ball. You want to avoid cracks in the dough. Press each ball down on a clean work surface and roll out to a small circle, about 4in (10cm) in diameter. It should not be too thin. Pour some cold oil in a bowl and rub the top of each disk with a layer of oil as you roll it. This will make it easier to roll. Transfer each disk to a tray when rolled and cover with a cloth to prevent it drying out.

When you are ready to fry, heat a 3-in (7.5-cm) depth of oil in a *karai*, or deep, heavy-based pan, over a medium heat. Fry one *lutchi* at a time, if you are new to it. Once you have practiced, you can fry two at a time. To test if the oil is the right temperature, take a small piece of dough and drop it in the oil—it should rise to the surface immediately. If it does not, the oil is not hot enough. Slide a *lutchi* into the oil from the side, do not drop it from the top. The *lutchi* will start to rise to the surface. Use a slotted spoon to gently push the *lutchi* down into the oil to make it puff up. Once the side in the oil has cooked, flip it over and cook the other side. The *lutchi* will remain pale, do not wait for it to darken to brown. Remove from the oil when both sides are cooked, to drain on paper towels. Repeat to cook the rest and eat warm.

*Pictured on pages 244–245*

# Khoobani Chutney

TANGY APRICOT, ONION, AND GINGER CHUTNEY

This tangy apricot, onion, and ginger chutney is a good accompaniment to any rich and complex meat or vegetarian main dish. The combination of thinly sliced ginger and onion is softened by the addition of slivers of dried apricots and brown sugar. The addition of tamarind tilts the balance of flavors of this chutney, from sweet and spicy to tangy and sour. This chutney will keep in a container in the fridge for a week. The main risk to this chutney comes from using a wet spoon to remove it, so avoid adding any water to it when you serve it.

5 tbsp vegetable oil

1½ tsp black mustard seeds

4 dried red chiles

1 tbsp raw cashew nuts

¾ cup (200g) shallots or pickling onions, thinly sliced

1 tsp ground turmeric

5oz (150g) fresh root ginger, peeled and thinly sliced

3½oz (100g) dried apricots, thinly sliced (this can be substituted with any other dried fruit or raisins)

2oz (60g) tamarind pulp (or 2 tbsp store-bought tamarind concentrate or purée, or to taste)

1 tbsp cider vinegar (or white wine vinegar)

1½ tsp salt

6 tbsp (75g) brown sugar or jaggery

Heat the oil in a deep saucepan over a medium-high heat until shimmering. Add the mustard seeds and dried red chiles, stir, and wait until the mustard seeds stop popping. Add the cashew nuts, and stir until they darken a few shades. Add the sliced shallots, and stir for 4–5 minutes until brown and caramelized. Add the turmeric and stir for a few seconds, then add the sliced ginger and apricots. Keep stirring for a couple more minutes, then add the tamarind pulp, vinegar, salt, and brown sugar or jaggery. Reduce the heat to low, and keep stirring until the excess moisture has reduced, and the chutney has a glaze. Cool and transfer to a clean jar with a lid, or a resealable plastic container, and store in the fridge.

*Pictured on pages 244–245*

# Index

# Acknowledgments

This book honors the man who instilled in me the rhythm and grace of Sufi music and poetry. My beloved teacher, guide, ustad, and father, Farrukh Said Khan. My love of the transient seasons, birdsong, and the beauty of the monsoons come from his prosaic stories and fables. The first year my children were in India in monsoon season, he initiated them to the family ritual by holding their hands and taking them out into the open courtyard in the pouring rain. Forever in my heart—monsoons are about home.

This book would not have been possible without the recipes of my mother. I am grateful to her for continuing to teach me how to cook all these years after she taught me my first dish. To my sister Amna and sister-in-law Shaista, my children Ariz and Fariz, my niece and nephews, Farhan, Faraz, Zynah, and Zahaan, thank you for your support. Thank you Wincie, for being my anchor! I am indebted to my amazing team at Darjeeling Express. Without the support of Asha, Damian, and Mario, this book would have been impossible to finish. Last but not least, I want to thank my husband Mushtaq and cat Bagha. By mostly ignoring me and my chaotic existence at home you have given me the space and unspoken support to thrive and find my path to happiness! I also want to mention my dearest brother Arif, who did not live to see this book. I know you would have loved the picture of your family around our childhood dining table—the table on which we spent hours playing table tennis as children.

I am delighted I got a chance to work with Paul Kelly and the formidable DK Red team. Thank you to my commissioning editor Cara Armstrong, the wonderful Tania and Izzy, Helen and Emily, and Emily Preece-Morrison. I am very grateful to Patricia Niven for the beautiful food photography, and to Annapurna Mellor for the location pictures. To Tabitha Hawkins for always knowing which plate fitted each dish and the super-talented Valerie Berry, whose calm, precise way of cooking ensured that all the recipes worked! Finally, I want to thank Ariz Khan for his support from the very start of the book and seeing it through to the very end with me, from helping with the recipes to editing them.

# About the Author

Asma Khan is the owner of Darjeeling Express, London, and one of the UK's most prominent female chefs. She comes from a royal background—Rajput on her father's side and Bengali on her mother's—and moved from India to Cambridge in 1991 with her husband. After feeling homesick, Asma first started to learn to cook with an aunt in Cambridge. After her aunt died, she returned to India for a few months to continue lessons with her mother and the family's cook. After returning to the UK and training as a lawyer in London, Asma founded a supper club in 2012. After great success, Darjeeling Express opened its doors in 2017 and became a critically acclaimed restaurant. She has been revolutionizing the London restaurant scene with her world-renowned Indian food, all-female team, and her commitment to training immigrant women.

In 2019, she was the first British-based chef to feature on Netflix's Chef's Table, and was named #1 on the list of 100 Coolest People in Food and Drink by *Business Insider*. She has since been named on the *Standard*'s Progress 1000 list; The *Vogue* 25, as one of the most influential women in 2020; and on *The Times* 100 List of the Most Influential People of 2024. She is an Honorary Fellow of Queen's College, Oxford, and serves as a Chef Advocate for the UN World Food Program, where she advocates for global food security, and helps raise awareness about hunger and malnutrition. Her work with the WFP aligns with her broader commitment to social change, and her focus on empowering marginalized communities, particularly women.

Asma's first cookbook, *Asma's Indian Kitchen*, won the UK category for Indian cuisine for the Gourmand World Cookbook Award, while her second cookbook, *Ammu*, won The Times Book of the Year award in 2022. *Monsoon* is her third cookbook. You can find Asma Khan online at @asmakhanlondon.

DK LONDON
**EDITORIAL DIRECTOR** Cara Armstrong
**PROJECT EDITOR** Izzy Holton
**US EDITOR** Sharon Lucas
**US EXECUTIVE EDITOR** Lori Cates Hand
**SENIOR DESIGNER** Tania Gomes
**SALES AND JACKETS COORDINATOR** Emily Cannings
**SENIOR PRODUCTION EDITOR** David Almond
**SENIOR PRODUCTION CONTROLLER** Stephanie McConnell
**ART DIRECTOR** Max Pedliham
**MANAGING DIRECTOR** Liz Gough

**EDITORIAL** Emily Preece-Morrison
**DESIGN** Eloise Myatt, Evi-O.Studio
**PHOTOGRAPHY** Patricia Niven, Issy Croker, Annapurna Mellor
**PROP STYLING** Tabitha Hawkins
**FOOD STYLING** Valerie Berry
**FOOD STYLING ASSISTANT** Eden Owen-Jones

First American Edition, 2025
Published in the United States by DK Publishing,
a division of Penguin Random House LLC
1745 Broadway, 20th Floor, New York, NY 10019

Copyright © 2025 Dorling Kindersley Limited
25 26 27 28 29 10 9 8 7 6 5 4 3 2 1
001–345242–Mar/2025

A catalog record for this book
is available from the Library of Congress.
ISBN 978-0-5939-6158-2

Printed and bound in China

www.dk.com